SELECTED LETTERS
OF
ALBERT JAY NOCK

Selected Letters of

Albert Jay Nock

collected and edited

by

FRANCIS J. NOCK

with

Memories of Albert Jay Nock

by

RUTH ROBINSON

THE CAXTON PRINTERS, LTD.

CALDWELL, IDAHO

1962

Printed and bound in the United States of America by
The CAXTON PRINTERS, Ltd.
Caldwell, Idaho
94032

To the memory of AJN and those
other "thrice precious, pockified blades"
who have departed this world.

R. M. T.

FOREWORD

During the last year or so of his life AJN worked on a manuscript of letters, with the intention of having them published. These were copies of letters sent to friends and correspondents subsequent to the publication of his *Memoirs of a Superfluous Man* in 1943. This manuscript was turned over to my brother and me after his death.

After a careful reading we both had the same feeling. The letters, like everything else written by AJN, were of a high order of literary merit. Yet it was obvious that, on the whole, they were a rehash of much of the material of the *Memoirs*, they were repetitive, and many sounded as if they had been written for publication. This last is borne out by a remark to one correspondent that the two should exchange opinions and views with the idea of subsequent publication. The letters shed no further light on any of AJN's ideas and convictions, nor did they present him to a possible reader in any way that he had not already presented himself in his previous writings. We both felt sincerely that it would do his memory a disservice to have the manuscript published. To avoid seeming too presumptuous we asked the opinions of others, and these confirmed us in our own.

We then agreed that a volume of AJN letters would nevertheless be in order. I tried to collect as many letters as possible with a view to have them edited. The results of my efforts were pleasing and also disappointing. Bernard Iddings Bell, Henry L. Mencken, Ruth Robinson, Paul Palmer, for example, had kept practically every letter, if not every letter, received from AJN. Other people sent me letters of his in answer to my request published in the New York *Herald Tribune*. How-

ever, many letters seem to be irrevocably lost. My mother
kept none, and neither my brother nor I kept as many
as we perhaps should have. Mrs. Hendrik Willem van
Loon wrote me that her husband had never kept any
letters after answering them; I have never been able to
find trace of the letters to Brand Whitlock beyond the
two or three of which Ruth Robinson kept copies; when
I wrote to Francis Neilson, I received a small number of
letters dealing with the beginnings of the *Freeman,* but
most of that correspondence seems to be gone; I could
not get on the track of a single one of the many letters
he must have written to correspondents in England after
his first trip there in 1911. Others who may have letters have not responded to my requests. To all who sent
me letters to copy I wish to express my sincerest thanks,
even when the editing forced me to leave them out of
the collection.

Of the letters, those to B. I. Bell, to Henry L. Mencken,
and a few others came to me in the original. The re-
mainder, especially those from the manuscript, those to
Ruth Robinson, to Paul Palmer and to Lincoln Colcord,
were typed out and sent to me. Thus I have not seen
the originals of some of the letters included in this collection, but the style and internal evidence show to me
that they are the genuine article. The manuscript, furthermore, is one with changes and corrections done in
AJN's own unmistakable handwriting.

When I had collected as many letters as I could we
asked Catherine Wilson to edit them. She declined, and
it was with some reluctance that I undertook the job.
The immediate problem was to decide what form the
collection should take. I felt that publishing all the letters available was out of the question; it would have
assumed too massive proportions. A selection made to
expound AJN's ideas and beliefs would have resulted
in a manuscript very similar to the one we had decided
against.

After looking carefully through them two or three
times I found that a selection and editing was possible
which would show, as none of his published writings do,
his development during the period from 1910 to the final

formulation of his philosophy of life as set forth in the *Memoirs*. Furthermore, it would be possible to show him as the human being that his friends knew and liked, to show that he was not always the "cantankerous old curmudgeon" that so many thought him to be because of his published writings.

In a letter from the last year of his life he wrote: "Damn all these doting relatives and timid editors, why can't they keep their wretched meddling fingers off, and let a man's letters stand as written?" This increased the feeling of guilt which I already had at the thought of editing his letters. For I already knew how he disliked having people know anything about him. Yet I believe his memory is better served by giving people an insight into him as a human being than by preserving the shroud of secrecy he always tried to keep about him.

Therefore, I selected letters with this double goal in mind and in many instances deleted portions of letters which would have served no purpose if published. I tried to avoid the charge of being doting or timid, although at times his remarks are very open to misinterpretation by some one who did not know him and hence did not know what he really meant. For instance, in one letter (not included here) he writes that he does not think he will go to see Paul Robeson as Othello. He adds: "I understand that he is now the big dinge down there." That happens to be the remark of a man who does not think that because something is done by a colored person it is *ipso facto* wonderful; it is furthermore expressive of his disgust over people who have such a thought and gush accordingly. It does not mean he was against colored people or their acting.

AJN has been accused of being anti this and anti that. To me only one thing is definite. He was against people he found unpleasant (and he found many to be such), avoided them as much as possible, and was likely to express his distaste. But the unpleasantness had nothing to do *per se* with race, color, or any other such characteristics.

As a small boy I came home from school and told him how several of us had plagued the Sicilian women from

the adjoining town. These women appeared with the
first dandelions each spring and cleaned out all the
lawns and vacant lots of our town. Several of us stood
one day and shouted, "Guinea, Guinea, Guinea!" at them
at the tops of our voices.

AJN took me in hand very gently and in a kindly
but firm way indicated to me that that was a pretty
poor performance. He pointed out to me that they were
different, poorer perhaps, but nevertheless every bit as
much human beings as we were who yelled at them. He
asked me how I would like to have to go among them
in their town and be the butt of their ridicule. It was
a lesson I never forgot.

About 1910 AJN came to New York to try his for-
tunes as a writer. He very soon became a member of the
staff of the old *American Magazine*. He quickly showed
his abilities as a writer, also his ability to straighten
out an editorial office. Some of his trips were taken at
the invitation of other periodicals to help them out. When
the *American* was sold and became a popular magazine,
AJN finally landed on the staff of the *Nation*. Then
he and Francis Neilson had their famous experiment
with the *Freeman*, which lasted for four years. After
1924 he never again allied himself with any periodical
beyond agreeing on two or three occasions to conduct a
department without having anything else to do with the
editorial policy. These occasions were of brief duration.

The period from 1910 to 1920 is represented almost
exclusively in this collection by letters to Ruth Robinson.
Also the letters to Brand Whitlock and to Ellery Sedgwick are from copies made and kept by her. Yet a fairly
clear picture emerges of AJN which is different from
that of the *Memoirs*. In addition we can follow a slow
course of disillusionment, a gradual realization that the
human race is not moving on beautifully to an ultimate
Utopia.

In 1911 he could write: "You'd hardly have me give
up the fight for economic justice, would you, in case I
get around in working trim again?" Yet eventually he
contented himself with pointing out what he felt the
nature and source of economic injustice to be; he no

longer wanted to fight for economic justice, as he felt that it was futile with humans constituted as they are. The letters from Milwaukee in 1913 show clearly his disappointment in the Socialist party there, a long step in the direction of refusing to believe that any party can bring salvation. Very soon after this, in January, 1914, he became quite vituperative over the treatment of labor at the Calumet, Michigan, copper mines. When he visited the region, he received another cold and sobering shower. In his own words: "Conditions of labour have been shockingly misrepresented. . . . There is plenty to say about the situation, giving everybody full credit all round, without telling such horrid falsehoods."

There is a similar contrast in feelings when we compare what he had to say about Germany in the early years of World War I with his *Myth of a Guilty Nation*. It is also ironical to read in his letters from London in 1915 of his hopes that humans will see the folly of war.

Perhaps the most astonishing thing to those who knew only the AJN as he was in later years was his apparent willingness to have something to do with politics. Some time after the first World War he mentioned to me that some friends had suggested that he run for Congress. When I asked him what he had said he told me that he had replied with Artemus Ward's classic line, uttered in the same situation, "My friends, dostest think I'd stoop to that there?" And in his letter to Brand Whitlock of August 27, 1912, he indicates clearly that he thinks a political party is no better than its leader.

Yet when Brand Whitlock suggested to AJN that he might get him a political appointment (December 31, 1912), he thinks it would be a fine thing for him. In a letter of September 9, 1913, he seems not completely averse to making campaign speeches. In Woodrow Wilson's second presidential campaign he even speaks of "putting myself forward for service in a political campaign" and expresses belief that this time politics does matter (September 20, 1916). Ten days later he writes that work has interfered and continues: "The disappointment is that it won't leave me very much time to save the country by being a politicker, and I had quite set my heart on that. However, perhaps I can work in something at odd times; only I had rather 'lowed as how I would give up these six weeks to helping Woodrow."

When it is remembered how violent he was on the subject of governmental interference in any way but to prevent and punish crime and to enforce contracts, it is also rather startling to read (September 4, 1914): "You asked me what I thought of setting up parks and playgrounds in a city by private gift. They should be municipal institutions in a complete sense,—a public investment that the city puts its money into because is very much worth while to do so. Our theory of municipal life is changing very much and at present it is in an anomalous condition. I think every private gift of this kind tends to blunt the city's sense of duty and corrupt its self-respect."

If in two or three places I have included a rather long letter expounding ideas expressed in the *Memoirs* and elsewhere, it is because there is nevertheless a strong personal touch which makes these expositions differ in quality from his published ones. In dating the letters I have been consistent in the form: month, date of the month, year. AJN was by no means consistent. He did usually place the date before the month, but he indicated the latter with the name capitalized and uncapitalized and with the Roman numeral. He usually did not put down the year, and when I have supplied this I have done it in square brackets. Other inconsistencies I have retained.

However, it is high time for a doting relative to let AJN speak for himself, first expressing gratitude to Robert M. Thornton and to The Caxton Printers, Ltd., for making this volume possible.

F. J. N.

University of Illinois

SELECTED LETTERS
OF
ALBERT JAY NOCK

SELECTED LETTERS OF ALBERT JAY NOCK

To Ruth Robinson[1]

PORTLAND, OREGON, January 16, 1911

Is this good,—or poor,—or bad?

> I am grown tired of city wretchedness,
> The little boys who swarm the stony street,
> Their thin, weak hands alert for bread to eat;
> The girls with hollow cheeks gnawed by distress,
> Who tread the bitter way: the selfishness
> Of ease, the pattering sound of drunken feet;
> Children still striving grief with mirth to cheat,
> And Death already on the puny chest.
> I can endure the gray, unholy hags,
> Though I must think the time when they were pure,
> And all the stumbling of the downward chase.
> I can endure the drunkard's hopeless rags,
> The squalid garrets of the wistful poor,
> But not, O God, the children white of face.

I think it is pretty good, though I can't judge very well.

But have you, oh, have you read "An Excursion to the Forest Belt"—Tourgueniev? If you have not gotten to it yet, look at the last three pages and tell me if there was ever anything like it. I reread that and Asya and Yakov Pasinkov today, and their old influence was redoubled. Oh, don't let anything keep you from them, and from the rest.

---

[1] A close friend of about the last thirty-five years of his life, who, among other things, did the delightful illustrations for his *Journey Into Rabelais's France;* a resident of Washington ("South") County, Rhode Island.

I was to go to Seattle today, but there is a train at midnight, by which I will lose no time there, and I can spend this whole evening here quietly reading; and that I will do.

I thought of telegraphing you to go & hear the cast of *Rigoletto* Saturday night, so that you might tell me of it,—but I didn't. Children of impulse, men & women of restraint, what fools we are, we grown-ups. I wish I could form a compact with some one (not you) to obey impulse & live by it for one week, unrestrained, without a single motive an inch below the surface. What a clearing, self-realizing, happy experience it would be. That will be one such attractive thing about Heaven,— we'll all do that all the time, & go right, just as we would go right if we did it here. But you are against this doctrine, I know.

I'll mail this from Seattle in the morning and you will know I'm there.

NEW YORK, March 26, 1911

You spoke about books & I must not forget them; so I am writing in order that you may keep this as a memorandum.

I urged Matthew Arnold's essays on you largely because they are an introduction to nearly all the good literature there is. The more you read him the more you will be drawn into the examination of other writers whom he speaks of. And the way he speaks of them always gives you the right handle to take hold of them by.

But there are a few others that I might mention, since you do me the honour to suggest it.

For books to keep beside me & turn to at odd moments, I would like to have you try Long's translation of Marcus Aurelius, the *Theologia Germanica* (Macmillan), a little of *Les Miserables*, about a hundred pages, namely Books I & II. I don't care whether you ever read the rest of it or not; but I very much want you to read this much, and read it very often.

I get enormous benefit from continually reading two

books of the Apocrypha—*Ecclesiasticus* & the *Wisdom of Solomon.* Perhaps you would prefer to make your way towards them by gravitation, as you would towards Emerson; but the best of the Hebrew spirit is there, & its great depth & value impresses me more each time I read it.

It is highly important to get command of at least one literature beside one's own. I see that a young French novelist has come forward with a plea for the study of the *foreign soul.* This is really necessary. Not that the soul is different from ours, as you of course know; but the difference in environment, in national spirit &c. creates shades of contrast. This is why I recommend the Russians to you so persistently; and in that connexion I wish you would get Kropotkin's History of Russian Literature & read it, as a framework for your books in that language.

Of course, you might get much the same result from reading Lessing, Herder & Goethe as from the Russians. But not nearly so well, for there is not the same freshness of presentation. I hope some day you will read Lessing's *Emilia Galotti,* anyway, and *Wilhelm Meister.* Goethe's *Conversations* is a book that you should always have by you, by all means.

I don't like to seem supercilious, but really, our contemporaneous English fiction is so fantastic & uncertain that I read almost none of it. One's time for reading is so limited that it seems one might best spend it upon what one knows is good rather than take chances on what one is not sure of. You would take great pleasure out of a modern book that is little known, called the *Apologia Diffidentis,* published by John Land; & I want the pleasure of giving you a little book by Max Muller next time we meet, called Memories, unless you already have it, or would prefer to have it otherwise than by gift.

I don't feel very sure of myself in recommending books to you, as I never had anything to do with a young lady's reading, & I'm not very well able to enter into your consciousness, with its inclinations and desires. So I am only advising in a general way & quite likely to make mistakes.

But you can dip into the books I speak of & if they do not find you, you can withdraw easily. The mere bulk of what one reads amounts to very little by comparison with the value of assimilating what one reads, even though it be not very much.

Editorial rooms of the American Magazine
NEW YORK, June 21, 1911

You'd hardly have me give up the fight for economic justice, would you, in case I get around in working trim again? I didn't understand your letter so, but it might have meant that.

"Be steadfast in thy covenant & the conversant therein, and wax old in thy work." Oh, that wonderful wisdom literature in the Proverbs & Apocrypha! That's what you meant to tell me, wasn't it? All right, I'll do my best,—my best isn't much just now but maybe it will be better. I'll try and have it so. I just said good bye to my mother,[2] & found out once more what a splendid sport she is,—she never winced, although I'm all she has in the world. I wish I could profit more by all these good examples I have around me. How wonderful they are.

PARIS, FAUBOURG ST.-DENIS, October 13, 1911

I got your last letter today, most appropriately on my birthday, for this is the day when I make another long step towards old age. I had just drifted down through Germany back into France again. You should by this time have received a letter I wrote you from Berlin, giving rather a meager & matter-of-fact account of my subjective experiences,—at least, we'll call them that. I do not think I will go down to the Puy-de-Dome again, —I do not yet at least, experience the inward admonition. Perhaps I will be turning my face homeward soon, perhaps not. But anyway, you will be informed.

---

[2] As he was leaving for Europe.

You were characteristically over-generous in saying that *I* was right, for the question of *who* is right is a very small one indeed beside the question of *what* is right. And I am so glad that your returning health has brought you another vision of the inner life. The objective experience of men & women in America does not give one naturally and habitually the view of human beings that one ought to have. One can get it, of course, but one has to work for it a little. In England one gets it least easily of all,—so it is all the more satisfaction to find it when it comes.

But on the Continent it is very different. I have been thrown with all sorts & conditions of men, and the display of their humanity has been like the unrolling of a celestial panorama. How I could write about it, if I only *could* write.

It has been the most impressive thing I ever experienced, to talk with the great benefactors of the race,—Archenhold the astronomer, Metechnikoff, Rathe, Grassi, Blaserna, Sir William Ramsay, Borel, Vinogradsky,—and discover their perfectly transparent simplicity, their cordiality and friendliness. Then on the other hand, you see exactly the same thing among the people you meet on the streets of the city & the lanes & roads of the country. It is wonderful, the friends one makes. The same mail that brought your letter brought a long one from my dear friend di Angelis of Turin, telling me of a deep domestic affliction. He was writing at three in the morning,—think of it, when I had known him only a week face to face, and will probably never see him again. I wish you could read that letter; it would be so convincing and confirming. Then I wish you might have been with me when I was talking with a young Russian girl of Taultchine in the government of Podolsk. I met her in a shop. I had to buy something and being unable to speak Russian I was greatly helped out when this girl volunteered in German. After she had bought what she wanted we walked out together & bless me if she didn't take me home with her & introduce me to her mother & cousin. The cousin spoke German pretty well, but the mother not at all. They were as cordial &

interested as they could be,—kept me to supper—and afterward the girl & I walked about in the cool evening. She was the exact, the living type of Tatjana in *Eugen Oniegin*. Although nearly twenty, I could not believe I was not listening to a child. She told her dreams, the revelations made to her by the wind & trees, the water & sunlight, as artlessly & prodigally as an infant, & with the same utter freedom from self-consciousness. It was very wonderful.

But recollections like these crowd on me from every nook & corner I have visited. Do you know, I haven't seen any "sights", any antiques, cathedrals and so on? Some way, I couldn't make the time or the interest. But oh, the men & women,—and the *children!*

Perhaps when we meet again I can give you some idea of it in conversation. I will try,—but I can't be led into any more of it in a letter.

It is generous of you again, to say that I have helped you to make a revaluation of the nature of men & women. But without me you would have been led to it by the facts of life because it is happily in your nature to be discontented unless you get *at* the facts of life. This excellent discontent would have done the work; still, I am glad if I helped bring the change more quickly. Every one of us incurs a greater debt to some other than he can ever pay. God meant it so, I think, to teach us our solidarity. If you are in debt to me, I do not realize it; but the sense of it will move you to pass the gift along to many another with big interest. I am in debt to many people—so very many. They are not aware of it and I can not possibly do anything for them. But the consciousness of it keeps tightening up the sense of humanity that always tends to work loose, more people fall into my range of action, and that is the way that the Lord of the harvest gets his "returns" in the long-run, and the way he intends they should come. Everything in our life teaches us to take a less & less *personal* view of our privileges & responsibilities; and that is the great ideal. I have told you before how one of the most over-powering ideas in the New Testament is, But I say unto you, &c. . . . *that ye may be the children of your Father which is in heaven,*—because, in other words, it is truly *natural* for a human being to do those things. And the farther one goes the more clearly one sees from the facts of life that it simply *is so.* If any one had followed me around only these few months, he would have seen so many people who had been born again to the purity & the simplicity of infants that he would not doubt it.

But this is a pretty heavy strain for a letter. I was an opera feller one night in Berlin,—*la Traviata* sung in Italian, happily, though by Germans. Jadlowker whom you remember in New York was Alfredo and Hempel sang Violetta. She is coming over this winter, I understand, & will have a great run with us, I'll wager. Much of the Mary Garden kind of thing, you know—can't sing & is none too well thought of here, but seems to have the sort of semi-physical semi-psychical attraction that affects vulgar minds. So she will do well. I was somewhat touched by the duet in the first act, but not so much I think by the present performance as by the memory of bygone ones. If I could only have heard Accobi & Brambilla sing it at Milan—or Lipkowska & Davidov at St. Petersburg—I would have had a fresh memory to take home with me.

PARIS, October 14, 1911

Rain, and 100,000 paniers full of blue devils coming in by window & door & down the chimney. This is such a depressing place,—like New York. So conspicuous a portion of it is given over to the sterile industry of making vice look innocent,—and it *won't.*

People are such asses. You always hear that in Paris, sensuality is so gloriously upholstered with amenity & nickel-plated with grace & attractiveness that it really isn't vice any more. Well, there is nothing in it. I have seen the *feu-follets* (will o' the wisps) as they are heartlessly called, in every city from Turin to St. Petersburg, and they are the same everywhere, poor souls,—and their business the same,—exactly as poor, as miserable and unhappy here as everywhere.

I had a very curious experience with one of them in London one afternoon. Remind me of it when we meet, —and another in Genoa.

No, I won't go back to the Puy de Dome. I can imagine what it would be in the browning haze of autumn, but as I said, I do not have the *intimation,*—rather, I have the intimation not to go. Don't imagine I am growing superstitious or any more impractical than I always am. Some day I will be moved by the same impulse in some direction, but not now.

I have quite clearly decided to come home. Perhaps a few days more in the country, perhaps a glance at the Breton coast. But if my days are prolonged beyond Mamma's I will come here to live, unless some other duty claims me, which is not likely. I have had many dreams of a permanent resting-place at Saint-Saturnin, making occasional excursions into the world to find the substance of things to write about and then returning there. As far as one can see ahead, which is but a little way, I expect to do that,—expect to work, and not lose myself in dreams. I learned a great deal about myself & what I ought to do in that fifteen minutes (perhaps, or more or less) on the Perspective Newsky. You need not fear but that I will work,—only I know I will work better here.

What a world of power there is in associations re-called by a strain of music. I have been haunted all day by that air from *La Traviata* (the *Un di felice eterea*), and tonight at dinner the orchestra struck up a most pleasing little melody called the *Valse Septembre,* —rather popular, no doubt you know it. The first time I heard that was on the steamship coming over; and for a moment I reproduced the whole original situation, —people's faces, fellow-travellers never known & quite forgotten—with photographic accuracy and tremendous power.

When the men of science have said all their say about the human mind & heart, how far they are from ac-counting for all their phenomena, or from answering the simple, vital questions that one asks them! What *is* the power by which a certain number & order of air vibrations is translated into processes of great emotional significance? If any one can answer that question believe me, he is just the man I want to see.

NEW YORK, April 4, 1912

Another large and busy day—plenty of things happening. Four of us together at lunch today at the Players' Club—Phillips, Baker, Boyden[3] and I—talking chiefly about the great issue of labour & unemployment. God! it is great to be alive at this time of the world. In spite of the misery & inequalities & heartbreaks I would rather live *now* while things are *"doing"* than hereafter when so many of them are all done. If the Lord spares us, you & I are going to have some splendid vigorous years and rejoice in them all.

BRANCHVILLE, April 8, 1912

I didn't get down to see George today, nor yet did I put in the rest of my fly-screens. It has been cold as charity, and I stuck pretty close at home working over my Tarbell[4] article &c wondering how well my coal is going to hold out. I stiffened up the furnace fire last night, & bless me if I didn't discover a great big steel-blue wasp flying around the sitting-room this morning. It gave me the hypo, but I finally mustered courage to kill it with a folded newspaper & then sat down and trembled violently for the balance of the morning.

I'm genuinely interested in writing about Miss Tarbell, and while I haven't made up my mind to print my stuff yet, I'm going to get you to run over it with me to see whether it's all there. Really, there is not much to say. When one has simply declared one's philosophy, all the details seem to fit in of themselves. My philosophy premises that women are not a sex by themselves, any more

---

[3] Of the *American Magazine* staff.

[4] Ida M. Tarbell, who wrote the history of the Standard Oil Company, was also on the *American Magazine* staff.

than men are, but are human folks. I can't tell you
how it gets on my nerves to hear a woman say as la
Pervenche did, that "Jim is very good about letting me
do" so & so. I can't reconcile those concessions with my
ideas of personal liberty. I say in this article, "Either
a woman is a human being or she is not. If she is, what
am I that I should pretend to control, regulate or dic-
tate another human being's conduct? If she is not, why
should I be interested in her companionship?" Of course
the real theory of the thing is proprietary—the man pays
the bills. That's the long and short of it.

But dear me, think of its being only fifty years since
chattel slavery was a matter of course. No doubt fifty
years from now women and men will be walking along
in relations of full justice and freedom,—the kind of
relations that people only idealize for themselves nowadays. The world will then be so much happier and
better when the services people render each other are
a free gift of good will and devotion. It's a great thing
to anticipate such a time.

To Brand Whitlock[5]

NEW YORK, August 17, 1912

DEAR MAWRUSS:

Yours of the 15th received and contents noted. In
reply would say I aint been on no vacation, Mawruss,
far from it. Fellers what sit on the end of the Narragansett Pier have their troubles too, I bet yer. I been
listening to a feller *schmooes* over scientific management,
Mawruss, a fat feller by the name Gilbreth. I didn't
buy no fifteen-cent cigars neither nor none of them—
now—sixty-cent ice-creams. I was at a hotel like one
of them two-and-a-half a day American plan houses out
in Ohio where I used to stop way before the Spanish
war already. Furthermore, Mawruss, I am surprised at

---

[5] This is an attempt to write the language of Abe Potash and
Mawruss Perlmutter, two fictional characters made famous at
that time by Montague Glass. Whitlock's letter, to which this is
the answer, is a much more authentic sounding affair.

you you should talk that way about my hay fever. When a feller abuses his partner and calls him a loafer yet because he got it hay fever and must got to stop and blow his nose oncet in a while, what a heart he got it, Mawruss! Like a piece from ice! Must I got to get your permission to get it hay fever, Mawruss? For anybody what's got such a nerve like you got it, Mawruss, I'm surprised you should make it such a poor reminiscer.

Now as far as I'm concerned, Mawruss, it dont make no difference to me when this work of yours comes in. If you dont do it in July you do it in August, and its all the same. But I also got it here a partner, Mawruss, a feller by the name A. Boyden, and no doubt you heard already what a cutthroat that feller is. If the goods aint in on time "sucker" is the least what he calls me, and when I tell him he shouldn't take it so particular he goes clear up in the air already. And if they are a week late, I would got it a better chanct if I lived in the next office one door by the other with some of them fellers up in Sing Sing. Such a show I should got it, Mawruss.

Remember me affectionately to Mrs. Whitlock, and believe me always your devoted partner,

ABE.

NEW YORK, August 29, 1912

DEAR BRAND WHITLOCK:

I got your letter of the seventeenth today, and everything in the photo line that you report sending is in and accounted for. Your correspondence with A. Boyden is a satisfactory memorandum of the business end of it as far as we are concerned, if it is to you.

But for Heaven's sake, Mawruss, what sort of talk is that about your holiday? You told me you would leave right after Labour Day and come on here, and I have all arrangements made for you, as I wrote early in the month. We'll have page-proofs out before you know it, possible rearrangements to meet the mechanical exigencies,—maybe some cuts,—and pictures to work in, and if you are off there in Michigan or in Toledo, smoking the K to M first-credit customers' cigars, we wont never get nowhere. I have an ideal place for you to work in undisturbed, near enough to me while I go on with the scientific management story, and also near enough the office so that we can get at you when necessary. I dont want to edit your stuff without you,—beside, we want to kill off as many of those infernal infancy-and-first-plug-hat pictures as possible,—and no end of other things, especially on the preliminaries and the first go-off. Bluffs you are making it. The sooner you arrive the better. Tell Washburn that October is out of the question. He can assemble those voters in late September just as well. Let me know about this right away, for the prospect of those page-proofs scares me to death.

I'm in a position of absolute neutrality on the Bull Moose party. With T. R. out of the way, one might be in it to the hilt; but never in the world as long as he is to the fore. The movement is a great deal bigger than he is, and in time it will come into its own. But at present, T. R. contains too many and too distinct possibilities of harm. I would not believe a single word he said under any circumstances whatever. I am sure he would have no hesitation about betraying and deceiving any man or set of men that trusted him, if it suited his purposes or favoured his ambitions to do so. I am willing to go on record publicly to this effect, if you or your friends can make use of my opinion. I recognize the advertising-value of his leadership in getting the thing launched, but *vilescit origine tali* is a sound principle, and the party will find itself in the long-run disabled and retarded by this means of temporary advantage. They trusted to the arm of flesh and not to principle for their initial carrying-power, and they will have to pay for it, in my judgment. I would be unfeignedly sorry to see you line up with them. I might recall to you Franklin's observations on the working-out of the party-principle, and I believe that now is the time above all for the true Liberals to remember how Socrates, according to Xenophon, said that in refraining strictly from any direct political activity he and his disciples were the only real politicians of the time. The opportunity was never so ripe for us to keep insisting that platforms and policies are only registrations, and poor ones at that, and to show that *Geist* is the only thing. Men will listen to that doctrine now, and take it in; just as they might in 1840-45 if there had been anyone to preach it. There is the chance for a smashing editorial on "A Refuge for the Liberal" to bring out this very point. The new party's principles are nearer mine than any other; but this is the prophet's age, not the mechanician's. The platform-monger has had a long innings, and the people are ready now to hear and learn. They are ready for the best that is in us, and it seems a pity to limit ourselves. Look at Wilson, as you say. He will be president, no doubt; but at what a sacrifice?

No, dont do it, old fellow. You have always made your works and ways tell towards the idea that politics are superficial,—and this new move as much as any. "The fashion of this world passeth away" Goethe said, when he reached our time of life, "and I would fain occupy myself with the things that are permanent." We have a chance to do that now as never before, through literature, speech and above all, life. I look for the same development in the present party-crisis as in the last, preceding the civil war, so long as the new party is content to submit to its present auspices. They will take up the tabernacle of Moloch and Chiun their images,—T. R.'s sombrero,—the star of their god Buncombe, and their hold upon the future will be correspondingly slackened. No, I have no stomach for it. I am wholly with Jones,[6] with Franklin and Tolstoy, in my estimate of parties; and while I will cooperate with every benign influence and help on every effort to "dispose us to a better sense of our condition" as Burke said, I wont do it under any aegis at present on the field or apparently likely to be set up there in the near future.

Dont fail to get on here as speedily as possible, Mawruss, for when those pages come out we want you near

---

[6] Samuel Milton Jones, known as "Golden Rule" Jones, mayor of Toledo 1897-1905.

at hand. Write me what you are really going to do. I can locate you ideally. I have everything fixed and my own time and engagements laid out to correspond. Let me know right away, for next Monday is Labour Day.

Affectionately, always,
Your partner,
ABE.

To Ruth Robinson

TOLEDO, December 31, 1912

The photograph business is about done with, & my stuff is being shipped off. Now for Detroit tomorrow evening, & then for Toronto, unless something changes the plan. I live in a very uncertain world all the time, but on this trip I seem to be in unusual doubt of just what I'm going to do.

Brand is getting out a sort of de luxe edition of his little pamphlet to the minister. He spoke today about getting me a foreign appointment under Wilson. What would you think? It would be a fine thing for me, but it seems a good way off, doesn't it?

Later

The goods have just been shipped off by express, & I have eaten a mouthful or two. I have had no appetite all the week, for some reason. Perhaps it is the miserable climate that gets into me. I might be writing an editorial, I suppose, if I felt more ambitious. But I'd rather chat with you. Later, I'll walk around the streets and see what this extraordinary Golden Rule city is like when the "lid is off." To hear the ministers talk, you would say that the whole population will go whooping to hell because the saloons will probably keep open an hour or so later than they did last night.

Yet I don't blame the ministers for their point of view. They can't see anything but the repressive side of morality. They always want to shut something up— the saloons, theaters, Sunday baseball & so on. My idea is always to open something. I want to start something instead of stopping everything. But they may be right and I wrong.

For that matter, wasn't I a daisy five or six years ago? How long it takes a being to become *human* under this infernal & devilish perversion of a social system that we call civilization.

I have been thinking about that foreign appointment. I don't know how Brand ever expects to get Wilson to appoint me even vice-consul to Baraboo, because I never did a hand's turn for the politicians & am no more a political Democrat than I am a hard-cider Prohibitionist; but for some reason he didn't seem to think there would be much trouble about it if I really wanted to go.

UNION CLUB, CLEVELAND
January 29, 1913

I got into Cleveland at six o'clock and found a note here requiring me to go to the banquet of the famous old Tippecanoe Society at seven. I had forgotten all about this being McKinley's birthday or I would have hidden in the woods. This Tippecanoe Society is a back-ribbed old-line Republican concern,—the most conservative in the world. The present condition of the Republican party was so much in evidence that it made the celebration rather a blue affair. Herbert Hadley of Missouri made a very good speech,—balancing between the new & the old like a rope-dancer, & trying to get a little of the new wine into the old bottles by making believe it was practically the same as the old stuff that always was there. I don't think he succeeded.

After I got there I was rather glad I went. It gave me a fresh insight into the afflictions of the politician even the good politician who has ideals of a certain order. He has to trim & cajole & work so much by indirection, that in the long-run he gets a pretty slippery turn of mind & a very low estimate of human beings. I can't think of anything more distasteful & impossible to me than public life. The time will come some day when a man can go into national politics with a sub-

lime disregard of parties & their claims, and get away
with it. Jones could have done it if he had lived. But
such men are very scarce & their absolute disinterestedness seems almost impossible to realize. Yet if one
can convince people of it, it is the quality that would
keep one in office, even now, more than any other. People
knew that Sam Jones didn't care a brass-mounted damn
about being mayor—so they kept him there.

It has snowed a little but the air continues warm &
the snow is only slush. I am here in the lap of the greatest magnificence, & rather enjoying it too. These old
sports are friendly & cordial & one likes their manners.
I suppose it is because we liberals are so superior to
everything that we fail in the smaller amenities that the
conservative is strong on. For the social courtesies and
minor loyalties of life, as well, give me the old fogy
every time in preference to radicals like, say, Louis Post
or Steffens, or indeed most of us. We are so taken up
with our general love for humanity that we don't have
time to be decent to anybody, as the conservative reckons
decency. Old Mark Hanna's picture is before me as I
write. He was a hard old citizen, but he was strong in
the little loyalties that radicals disregard. Radicals like
Sam Jones or Charles Williams[7] are different, of course;
but I'm speaking of the general run of us.

It is certainly a lesson we can learn from the conservative,—that it is the concrete person that ought to
engage our sympathy & loyalty. That is one of the
things that makes our friendship of such vast value to
me, & the chief reason why I instinctively always consider you as one of the real liberals of Jones's own type.
You love great principles & are fascinated by the un-
folding of a great philosophy, but you never let them
cloud your immediate perceptions of the individual person. You are always thinking of some one that you can
help and benefit. Louis Post and I would sacrifice ourselves for the single tax, & would help a fellow-being
if he came in our path; but we wouldn't get the unconscious affectionate simple kindness into our talk with

---

[7] Who wrote for the *American*.

some bum illustrator in a doctor's office that you do. That woman will always remember that contact, & so will every one you touch. That is the great thing after all. When I die, I may be remembered as a good liberal who helped the cause along, but not many are going to feel that they have lost a friend.

I left poor old Mawruss grunting, & cussing everything & everybody in the world. He is utterly miserable; and his condition reacts on me so badly that even this little run to Cleveland was a welcome change.

En route Detroit, Saturday morning
June 7, 1913

We have just left Toronto and are due in Detroit at 3:15 this afternoon. There appears to be a Presbyterian convention somewhere down the line, & I was mightily entertained by studying a raft of the delegates on the platform at Toronto. The North of Ireland Protestant type has been preserved in great purity in southern Ontario, & great numbers of them were out, men and women of angular and craggy build and with faces, Mawruss, hard like iron, y'understand, all ready to burn witches or assassinate the Pope. That is a merry party they will have, take my word for it, & I'm middling glad to be moving on, out of range.

They were regretting that I didn't come in Montreal the night before so I could have seen Prince Albert, one of 'is Majesty's youngsters who blew into the Place Viger off a training ship. To tell the truth, I wasn't as much interested as I might be in the chance of meeting 'is Royal 'ighness, because that family has been stationary so long that it has sort of petered out in intelligence—and I think I spent Thursday much more profitably, & I'm sure a great deal more pleasurably.

Well, I had a wonderful experience yesterday, & I wonder whether I can tell you about it. What will come of it I don't know, but it is possible that one of the biggest and best things in the world. You remember I told you I had a lunch appointment with one of the C.P.R.

officials. At lunch he talked very little and rather absent-
ly, & I pretty nearly made up my mind that Canadians
were more agreeable in their offices than when they
were chatting socially. He took me over the new station in a perfunctory kind of way, and then left me
abruptly, but asked me to come back to his office at five
o'clock, saying he would be through his work by that
time and wanted to see me. So I went there at five
o'clock & found him out, but he had left word for me
to wait. He came in about half an hour, told me that
his family was all away & that he disliked very much
to eat alone, & would I come out with him to dinner.
So we set out, & still he had very little to say all through
the meal, except that he mentioned two or three times
how glad he was to have me with him, & that he regarded me more as a friend than as a newspaper man
or publicist. Still he was reticent; but after dinner he
lay down on the sofa & evidently with his mind made
up to talk, he began & for an hour & a half he talked
rapidly & steadily, giving me his most intimate inside
views of the relations of the railroads & the public. It
was, I think, the most wonderful talk I ever listened
to, and as radical as it could be. Brandeis could not have
done better. He said he was sick & disgusted with
the defences put up by Brown &c McCrea, and as for
Mellen's[8] he said it was simply unspeakable; that the
public would never be fooled by them a moment, & that
the public would never be on good terms with the railways until the railways came right across with a candid
acknowledgement of their false position. And so forth
and so on.

Then he went down to the train with me & stayed
until I pulled out, after doing me some little favours
that saved me a heap of trouble. The last thing he said
was "I don't want a lot of money and a fancy house
with automobiles & racehorses, but I do want to feel

---

[8] William C. Brown, president of the New York Central Railroad;
James McCrea, president of the Pennsylvania Railroad; Charles
S. Mellen, president of the New York, New Haven and Hartford
Railroad and of the Boston and Maine Railroad.

that I have really done something that counted for the public service."

The practical thing is this. During the time I am away, this man will jot down notes & so will I, & we will correspond. Then I will come back by way of Montreal & we will put our heads together in a statement that will not be sensational, but candid, temperate & statesmanlike, embodying the substance of his conversation with me. Then we will take it in & use our best powers of persuasion & reasoning to get Sir Thomas Shaughnessy[9] to sign it & let it be published under his name. It seems almost too much to expect, that he will do this. But if he should, it would reverse the entire railroad policy of the United States. For widespread & far-reaching effect, such a statement coming from the president of the C.P.R. would put Wilson's inaugural out of the running. It would be the most clearing & calming & reassuring thing that has happened in these last chaotic twenty-five years.

GOLF, ILLINOIS, June 18
later

I wish our lot could be cast in Chicago next winter instead of New York. It is so much more interesting. And don't make any mistake about the sincerity of the Chicago people's attempts after culture. They are popularizing good music, art & literature—really popularizing them—as I don't believe they are doing in any other city. I am greatly surprised at the evidence of it. And really, life here is astonishingly wholesome. I know you would be pleased and interested and I wish we could work here next year.

Four women are sitting at my elbow discussing the reduction of flesh,—loafers. It is a curious thing how certain women can muster up quite intelligent conversation when talking with a man, & when they sit with a crowd of women they talk like absolute fools. I don't wonder, as Whitlock says, that men don't care to talk

---

[9] President of the Canadian Pacific Railway.

with any women except those who are in some vital contact with the world—stenographers, book-keepers and salesgirls, newspaper women & such like. I am very much amused by the relations that these men maintain with their wives. Friendly enough, but both husbands & wives are frankly bored & just tolerate each other while around. And dear me, it is no wonder. There has to be some kind of *interest*, not domestic or biological, to hold them together. Marriage looks to me a whole heap like an endurance test, and I think it is a pretty humiliating business. Ten or twenty years ago, it was about all there was, except for a few gritty souls; but nowadays, thank fortune, things are a bit easier. In five years more they will have enlarged a lot, and we will have a lot of cleaner lives & a lot less lying & hypocrisy. And what interests me most of all, women will develop some self-respect and character,—meanwhile, good Lord, what a poor sort they are!

AUDITORIUM HOTEL, CHICAGO, June 27, 1913

This place seems the only one that affords even the appearance of relief from the appalling heat. I have been sitting at a table on the outer balcony breathing in soft coal smoke & trying to imagine a breeze that does not exist, and thinking up a red hot article on prostitution & the white-slave traffic that I shall surely write if I never print it. I dread the idea of going away & going to bed; & yet I suppose I must shortly do that.

I have been getting madder & madder at the hysteria over these subjects until it seems to me I simply must write some kind of counsel of moderation. There is no doubt about it that we are in for a big mess of Puritanism all over the country. We have a Puritan in the White House & a Puritan Secretary of State,—and all down the line, Puritanism is disgustingly good politics just now.

I hate the thing myself, and more than that, I dread the reaction that is bound to come. Why can't we proceed quietly and philosophically, according to principle, and avoid an extreme in one direction that means an inevitable extreme in the other? And the most hateful thing about it is its intolerable meddling hypocrisy.

CHICAGO CLUB, CHICAGO, June 28, 1913

There is a very queer thing here this afternoon. A lake breeze is skirting the shore of the lake, and everything within a few hundred yards of the shore is cool & all behind that is blistering hot. The front of this club for instance, is very comfortable but the rear of it is like an oven. It's as strange a phenomenon as I ever saw.

After lunch today I went to my room at the U.C., got into my pajamas and wrote 2000 words on my prostitution-white-slave article. I never did better work in my life nor any as fast. 2000 words is a big day's work for me & I did it between 1 & 4:20; and it will need very little changing. I don't know that the article will be fit to print or that our magazine is the place for it. But I do know that it is rousing good stuff and has a sound philosophy behind it.

At 4:30 I dressed & came over here, sat in the window & read awhile, & now (7:45) I have just eaten a light dinner. This is the Union League Club of Chicago, and has a duplicate of ———— ———— sitting in every arm-chair,—a choice assortment of fine old crooks. I never enjoy these places because the servants watch you too closely for fear you will wait on yourself a little, and I hate being waited on & hovered over and so I get nervous. A very solemn man waited on me at dinner & stood behind my chair until I thought of offering him a dollar to go away & stand somewhere else; but he would have reported it & gotten my friends in trouble with the house committee. So I finished and fled as soon as I could.

The hay fever started in punctually this morning, and showed that it is right on the job. I got my smarting eyes to seeing straight by about ten o'clock, however, so it might have been worse. Monday will tell the story,

I think, of whether I remain here longer or flee up the lakes. With the stack of writing I have to do and the hay fever, I am thinking very favourably of a few days on the deck of a steamer, to tell the truth. If it would knock a week out of the period I have to suffer, it would be worth something to me, especially as I am feeling pretty jaded & rotten just now, anyway. I tell you, this trip has been a good deal of a siege in one way & another, even though I have quite a bit to show for it.

If I can find a copy of the English Review I want to send you an article on the white slave humbug. It is extremely clear & would be convincing to any but those who have an inflamed pathological kind of interest in the subject, like those slab-chested, shad-bellied old maids who made Whitlock's life a burden. I never told you that story, I think,—I tell it in this article.

I know you will think I am a very horrid man, but I have seen a great deal of the kind of lady who is so uncommonly anxious that the rest of the world should be very moral and proper, according to the standard set on Plymouth Rock. And I always suspect that the vices & shortcomings of other people would interest her very much less if four or five times a week the right man should get his arms around under her shoulderblades and make her think she had been caught flat on her back in a hay-press. The same is true of men. Any one who has persistently neglected or violated a natural instinct is mighty apt to find it ingrowing into something meaner & dirtier than white slavery. That is the reason why the Puritans, with all their virtues, earned the contempt of normal people.

So there now,—I suppose you are turning up your nose. But such are my suspicions.

To Ellery Sedgwick[10]

NEW YORK, August 9, 1913

DEAR ELLERY SEDGWICK:

I was very glad to get your note this morning, and to

---

[10] Editor of the *Atlantic Monthly.*

find that you were half way hospitable to the article I sent you. As I told you, I did not write it for publication and therefore did not take pains to search it for possible asperities. I will be very glad, indeed, to come up to Boston shortly and go over it with you, and modify it in any way we think necessary, in order measurably to have it win its way.

What I had in mind to write you and what indeed I am very desirous of printing in the Atlantic is a moderate showing of the distinction between vice and crime and the futility of all general laws. This, too, we can discuss when I get up there and meanwhile I will prepare a sort of sketch of what I want to say so you can advise me about its acceptability and add to it or take from it as you think best.

Of course, I realize that nothing must be written in the spirit of exasperation. That seems to be the feature of Mencken's writing which stands in the way of its getting itself accepted. Yet when one sees the distressing invasions of personal liberty and the abominable fence-building political machinations committed in the name of public morality by legislators of the type of Jim Mann[11] for example, it takes a steady editorial head to keep one's writing within the strict limits of sweetness and light. I count on you to supply the ballast and the balance.

I will come up to Boston pretty soon and give you due notice of my approach, so that you can arrange with the ice company for extra emergency delivery.

Faithfully yours,
ALBERT JAY NOCK

To Ruth Robinson
NEW YORK, September 9, 1913

Osborne is a candidate for Governor of New Jersey on the Progressive ticket,—or rather, he is out for the nomination against Everett Colby, who is the Roosevelt kind.

---

[11] Lawyer and Congressman from Illinois, author of the famous Mann Act.

I enclose his leaflet from which you can see that he is at the root of the matter. He seems to be a progressive of the type of Amos Pinchot & Billy Kent. This presents something of a temptation to me, because I am considering a reply to Osborne's communication asking for some kind of support. I would like to do something to signalize the fact of those principles being brought forward in an Eastern state campaign, and yet I have such indifference to any direct political action that I could scarcely accomplish anything that would help him much—and of course, like all the rest, I suppose, that is what he most wants. I dare say that I can manage something—maybe a speech or two, or a little summary of the tax situation here and in New Jersey. What I think I will propose will be to appear here & there just as a kind of expert opinion, keeping off the political aspects of the situation altogether, and then after I have talked about taxes, the regular spellbinders can come in & say what they like. This may not suit them, but if not, I can do it independently, anyway.

CHICAGO, October 26, 1913

Which always brings back the point that Tolstoy raises in his *What is to be Done?* I don't see how I can sympathetically serve the interests of the great mass of the people unless I can somehow get a more vivid sense of their situation & conditions. There is a quality that I miss in my own writing that might be supplied by a little different kind of experience. My stuff is good enough, perhaps, and surely better than five or six years ago, but it still sounds as though it was written from a seat in the grand stand. I remember with interest that my nearest approach to what I want to reach was in my Coatesville article, & that was the result of the vivid and terrible experience of being there. But I don't see how the mere change to earning my own living out of the ground would produce that quality. In fact, it would seem not to produce it at all. So I suppose I shall have to produce it some other way.

It is a very mixed up mess. I haven't so many years before me now that I can afford to waste very much time doing the wrong thing.

NEW YORK, November 20, 1913

After your train went out last Monday, I had occasion to go in to see my friend Charles H. Ingersoll who makes the wonderful two-dollar watch I carried, & mentioned to him that it wouldn't keep time; so he exchanged it for another which was worse. Returning today, I commented a little earnestly on this, and finally he persuaded me to take one of a better quality,—some new wrinkle in cheap watches, I believe, which is extraordinarily accurate. So I suppose when you see it, you will be very proud.

But really, I find that carrying a watch doesn't make me feel any more civilized & self-respecting; & I sometimes wonder whether your view of the matter is quite sound. I never needed a watch—never felt the need of it—always knew what time it was, near enough—and all I seem to have done is to take on the responsibility of an unnecessary nuisance. Why should one *learn* to depend on some new *thing,* when the inevitable burden of *things* is already very great? I always thought the complexity of the things we are used to, was rather against a happy life than in its favour. Am I right or wrong? If so, why try to get used to anything more, even a watch that has to be wound? I suppose one can carry the idea too far, but I always hated the dead weight of any kind of property that has to be taken care of without giving adequate return.

This winter I am going to take hold of my life pretty energetically and simplify it. Some of these days, one room twelve feet square is going to hold every dollar's worth of everything I own in the whole world,—not that I own such a heap now, you know, but what I do own is a deal more than I want to be bothered with or propose to be. And when you get tired of me as a hopeless case, I'm going to turn that Ingersoll watch over to some boy with a possessive instinct.

Ellery Sedgwick is in town,—he was in the office to-day, but I didn't see him. The boys had fun with him over my "quiet pleas for the unprincipled life." But as it happened John Phillips was looking into the last *Current Opinion* where there is the strongest support to everything I said in my white slave paper,—and more. What an aggravation it is that you can't read,—it is a magnificent honest article, practically a confession, by a man of large experience. It merely indicates the supreme silliness and hysteria we have been indulging in, just as I tried to do. I sent a line to Fred Howe, calling his attention to it. People will find before they are through, that Tolstoy put it all on a page & a half.

Woodrow still sits tight on the Mexican question,— and Bryan remains still the heaviest load the poor man has to carry. Twenty years of continuous outpouring at Chautauquas does dishevel a man,—no doubt of it. Bryan goes out of his way to embarrass the Administration even when it would be easier not to.

ALBANY, December 9, 1913

Well, I've had a bully good time here & made excellent friends and think the outlook on state politics is very encouraging. But I am really not sorry to get away, for after all, politics is nix. It's only a reflection. I leave for Montreal tonight and get there tomorrow morning.

A long talk with the Governor[12] deepened my regard for him. He is really very able & sensible and we will watch him with interest. He is extremely candid and very amiable, and I think thoroughly honest and energetic. He ought to be a national figure before he gets through.

There are lots of wonderful things to talk about,—it is a superb thing to be alive & on the job just now— but I must get my dinner now shortly and put my things

---

[12] Martin H. Glynn, who became governor when William Sulzer, the elected governor, was impeached and removed from office.

to rights. That trunk is a perennial joy. I went so far as to buy a metal cigarette-case today for 75c—so now I won't be toting those pasteboard boxes any more. I might have hinted at one from you for a Christmas present, but maybe I have fared better than I would if your thrifty eye had picked it out.

Albany has pretty girls—a good many of them. Their figures aren't so much,—rather spindling & slab-chested, & their feet seem to have been designed by the Cubists. But in general, I like their faces and their manners are mostly natural & pretty. You will see some real figures in Italy—even the little girls of fourteen or so stick out in front like pouter pigeons. I'll bet there haven't been fifty nursing-bottles sold in Italy in fifty years,— and that is something worth while.

MONTREAL, CANADA, December 10, 1913

I had a good night on the train after all. The car went smoothly & the schedule was slow, & I slept first rate; and here I have been all this day of driving snow, enjoying my old friend the Hotel Place Viger, but most of the time around at the Canadian Pacific offices.

There are not many folks here and all of them English. I imagine our dining-room today was some like the cabin of the Adriatic,—everything & everybody capable, efficient, rectangular and utterly devoid of charm or humour. I wonder who could love an Englishwoman. I dare say it has been done, but I wonder who did it and how. I have the same curiosity that I have about the kind of person who first ate a crab or an oyster. I have looked at those we have here, and thought of it a great deal. Maybe I will start some experiments on Westheimer's cigar-sign when I get home. I know to a certainty that if anybody can get an answering gleam or a thrill out of these women, I can make that wooden Indian respond like Galatea to Pygmalion,—believe me, I can. When I get the Indian eating out of my hand, maybe if business is slack I'll return here & court the ladies. Incidentally I believe Montreal is the only city in the world without one pretty woman in it. Of course, I haven't seen them all but I have seen a great many & those I have seen don't hold out a blessed ray of hope for the rest.

But I certainly am well treated here—as I somehow seem to be everywhere. What nice people there are, and how many there are! Today I was off & on with the man in the CPR system who occupies the same position as your friend Mr. Buckland does in the New Haven. He took me to dinner, & then came here with me & remained talking until 10:30. Tomorrow night he takes me to the opera,—*Carmen*, in French—and I don't think I'll hear the flower song as well done as it is on your record.

This chap is an Oxford man, also of the universities of Berlin and Aberdeen; & we talked of classical literature and real world-events. It seems so strange to find that sort of man in that sort of position,—but it isn't uncommon. Tomorrow he is going to give me an essay on Japan by Lafcadio Hearn and a volume of history of the Scotch colonies in Canada. He made the most interesting comparisons of Japanese culture with that of the ancient Greeks—I had never heard of the idea & it fascinated me.

MILWAUKEE, WIS., December 16, 1913
11 P.M.

This is a mighty nice hotel, but like all the buildings in the Middle West, apparently, they keep it hotter than the hinges of Tophet. The region is worse than Germany for hot houses & offices, & poor ventilation. The water hereabouts is all harder than Pharaoh's heart. I use a special hard water soap, but even that doesn't amount to anything. I bathe mornings just because it is a pleasant sensation,—it doesn't help me make a hit with the Board of Health. And as for drinking any of it, it is out of the question. One would have to chase it down with muriatic acid, like you use to clear the deposit out of the teakettle.

I got in at 8:30 tonight, and shall now go to bed & get in good shape to mix in with them way-up Socialists tomorrow. I think I have found out why they were defeated. They talked themselves out of office. People were pretty well satisfied with their government, but while they were in the saddle they had such a lot to say about the class struggle and cussing the capitalists, & were so thoroughly class-conscious that they alienated about 6000 votes that were friendly on general principles, & thus were wafted out of office by a current of hot air. Exactly so. Moral,—don't talk. Don't crowd the mourners. If people don't care for all your doctrines, but like your work, put the soft pedal on and keep busy. Aint it? But the 'way-up Socialist can't do that any more than he can fly, apparently.

I think I can squeeze in part of Sunday with Mawruss over in Toledo. It is a long ride to Montreal & I must be there bright & early Tuesday morning, the 23rd.

MILWAUKEE, December 17, 1913

I've been chasing up the record of the Socialists all day and I have a lot of notes to go over to get in shape before tomorrow; so if you think I can sit around & waste much time with you, you are mistaken. I'm just a plain labouring man now, and can't afford luxuries.

Well, this has been a discouraging job. I wanted to find a few good words to say for the Socialists, but I don't seem to see them coming. All one can say is that their administration was free from graft & bribery. They didn't initiate anything of any account, their main features being suggested by outsiders. They appear to have played politics as diligently as anybody, worked the spoils system for about all it was worth,—and worst of all, they have worked dead against every measure of reform that wasn't in the line of their party,—for instance, every measure of election reform and every democratic measure in charter-revision. I find that they have consistently opposed these on every occasion—such way-up Socialists they are. I have about half a dozen points

on my list—specific instances of the sort,—and I'm going to take them up with Victor Berger tomorrow and
ask why. I think it will be in a way rather good fun to
do that, although I am really quite disappointed because
I hoped I would have to revise my opinion of them,
which hasn't been favourable, as you know.

I am wholly incapacitated when it comes to understanding anyone's devotion to party. It would be impossible for me to get up the slightest party feeling or
the sense of any allegiance due to a party. There is
some consolation to know that Franklin and Washington
felt the same way. So it isn't likely you will hear of
my holding office very soon.

MILWAUKEE, December 18, 1913

Another beautiful sunshiny day—a little colder than
it has been, but not to hurt. Even snorting around for
two hours this afternoon in an automobile didn't chill
me through. The sunset was very gorgeous & beautiful.
I am pleased with the lay-out of the city,—and here, as
everywhere, I find such corking fine people. How many
of them there are, in every city from the Atlantic to the
Pacific, buckling in to do something, and succeeding!

But my errand here is a disappointment. I never took
any stock in Socialism and precious little in Socialists,
and I was in great hopes of finding that they had covered
themselves with glory. Nothing of the kind, unfortunately. I saw Victor Berger[13] this morning and Weber,
another one of their high lights, and couldn't get anything out of them at all, except a lot of declamation
against capitalists, reformers & everything & everybody except Socialism & Socialists. So I was a good deal
disheartened.

---

[13] Milwaukee journalist and socialist, first socialist elected to Congress.

BRANCHVILLE, December 26, 1913

I read Jack Reed's[14] poem that he printed in our magazine a couple of years ago, called The Wanderer to his Heart's Desire,—and more than ever I liked it,—

"You there—I here,
Not all the brightness of your face
Nor joy of your fair company
Can bring us to one place."—

and so on, five lovely verses. I know you read them when they were published, but I dare say you have forgotten them. Jack never did anything that I thought was as good.

Well, I have been a great idler today. It has been one of those frightfully chill, contracting, shivering days when Nebuchadnezzar's furnace would not keep you warm, and your soul & mind shrink to nothingness. I managed to write out 20 or more topics for the autobiography this morning, which was mere copying, & that is as far as my industry has gone. The weather has changed to a livable cold, however—a clear air, which is the great thing—and I think perhaps tomorrow I may have the ambition to tackle something. I have spent a good deal of the day visiting with our rural neighbours. This morning I sat in the post office a long time while the postmaster entertained me with scraps of philosophy picked up at his point of vantage. I have often compared life here—an hour and a half from New York —with life in the village of St. Saturnin,—five hours from Paris,—the little village where I once thought of going to settle down, without ever having seen it. After all, perhaps there is little difference. The people here know that I do something "outside"—something that takes me to a great many places and among many people, but I do not think many of them know what it is, or are interested to know. After dinner tonight I breasted the bitter air as far as a couple of the neighbour's homes,

[14] John Reed, poet and revolutionist; on the staff of the *American;* author of *Ten Days That Shook the World;* socialist, later Communist Labor Party member.

talked with them, and came back reflecting on the compensations of those who "are born, live, & die in the same place,"—and there are some, no doubt, and a tired man feels their force in a peculiar degree. After all, the big thing, as you told me when I first knew you, is to make good on one's job wherever & whatever it may be. One of these men tonight is an artist in woodwork, —an artist to an eminent degree. He showed me serving-trays and tables he had just been making in inlay-work out of mahogany & ebony & other fine woods, and I admired them greatly. He has pride in his work, and speaks of it with a pleasant simplicity & naturalness. Such things are an achievement.

BRANCHVILLE, December 28, 1913

I bet you can't imagine where I am writing this,—in the kitchen. My mother & I have just been nibbling & chatting here, and I was afraid my smoke might drift in her room upstairs & aggravate her cough, so I told her it seemed pretty cozy by the kitchen stove & I'd just bring my pen & ink down & scribble here for a few minutes. Her cold hangs on as tight as mine has.

Well, I think I'll go into town tomorrow and clean up my errands, as far as possible, being fairly well ahead with my work. I am on the homestretch with my Albany story for the Outlook, it only remaining to be seen whether the Governor approves of what I've said. I have put in "rentpayers and taxpayers" throughout and if he doesn't let it stand, there will be a fight. That's one thing we owe to Gaynor—his wide advertisement of the fact that rent payers as well as tax payers have a share in government. Some time I have thought I would go up to one of your benighted God-forsaken "taxpayers' meetings" what you got it, up in Rhode Island; and just take the skin off your system of denying representation to rent payers. It would be a distinct public service, I think.

Tuesday night, the 30th, I am going to the annual

dinner of the Intercollegiate Socialist society. It will be quite a large affair, so I suppose no one will have to speak unless he is a 'way-up Socialist. I will feel a good deal like a cat in a strange garret, but I want to see what the rising generation of Socialists looks like. I do not wonder at the increase of the movement. I saw by yesterday's paper that Mayer had been set upon in Calumet, & beaten, put on board a train & carried forcibly out of the state. Those tactics did not work in Lawrence, in Paterson, in Little Falls, or anywhere that they have been tried; but people are very slow to learn. And the number of Socialists enlarges daily in consequence.

But that is not the main point. Every day that is marked by that kind of thing increases the number of souls who substitute passion for reason, and makes less room for the dispassionate facing of the fact that they who take the sword shall perish by the sword,—which is as true of industrial weapons as military weapons.

It isn't with much interest that I face the prospect of going in. I feel rather out of sorts at having fizzled out on two editorials hand running,—but somehow I *couldn't* write them, & that's the whole story. Everything in town seems uncommonly alien & hateful. I am having one of my protracted fits of not being interested in anything. The fellows write letters, alternately cussing & encouraging me, but not to much purpose. Well, I may feel differently in the morning—there's always that chance, thank fortune.

NEW YORK, December 31, 1913

I wouldn't have missed that gathering last night for a great deal, as it was one of the most interesting I ever saw. The Intercollegiate Socialist Society is what its name implies; and I think there is a chapter in every college in the land. The dinner was held in the Murray Hill Lyceum at 34th St. & 3d Ave.—a very good place. There were about eight hundred persons present, mostly young, the sexes about evenly divided. I was absorbedly interested in studying their faces, some of them being among the most beautiful that I have ever seen, and all of them full of energy, intelligence & curiosity. There was a very magnetic spirit liberated among them. If a person couldn't make a good speech there he never could.

The dinner was fair, but I didn't pay much attention to it. I saw several old friends,—the Wallings, Rose Pastor, Max Eastman[15] & several others, among them George Lansbury, the Labour member of Parliament, who lost his last election by going in for suffrage. I was delighted to see him again. He was kind to me when I was in England.

Mrs. Charlotte Perkins Gilman[16] made the first speech, introduced by Max Eastman who was toastmaster. Eastman told me by the way that Jack Reed is in Mexico. Just like the boy to push in where it is coming thickest. I asked when he was coming back and Eastman said he guessed it depended on whereabouts he got shot.

Well, after Mrs. Gilman's speech, everybody sang Socialist songs, without much of an idea of singing. Then a couple of young collegians talked—a chap from Amherst who made a good impression and had memorized his speech; also a tall, frail & pretty daughter of Dean Kirchway of Columbia who had her speech written out but with such a good idea of it that she didn't use her manuscript much. Dean Kirchway isn't a Socialist & has no sympathy with it; but the girl is head mogul in the Barnard chapter.

Mrs. Harriet Stanton Blatch then took the floor for suffrage, and I had food for thought; also when Hillquit[17] spoke for Socialism. I realized again, as I have often & often before, how much more favourably one is impressed with the rank & file of any movement than by its constituted leaders. In my experience, this is true

---

[15] William English Walling, socialist and labor movement leader, and his wife Ann Strunsky Walling, also a socialist; Rose Pastor Stokes, a socialist leader; Max Eastman, at that time editor of *The Masses*.

[16] Lecturer and writer, particularly associated with the labor question and woman's rights.

[17] Mrs. Blatch was a social reformer, writer, and an advocate of woman suffrage. Morris Hillquit was a lawyer and author who ran for mayor of New York on the Socialist ticket.

of them all—the labour movement, Socialism, single tax, & above all, of woman's suffrage. When I talk with the average thoughtful woman I have no difficulty keeping my faith in them or in the justice of their assuming the right to vote. Opponents of suffrage do not make me have any misgivings, either. But a woman like Mrs. Blatch makes me harden my heart against all womankind. For the time being I would gladly see women reduced to the most abject condition of chattel slavery. She is intolerable, unspeakable.

In remarkable contrast with her speech and Hillquit's were Dubois,[18] the negro, and Lansbury. There were real leaders. Both were thoroughly alive, awake & in deadly earnest; but they gave the impression of being wholly disinterested, of seeking nothing for themselves, whether glory or credit or money. And how powerful that is! When you get that note in a man's speech, everything goes right up to a higher plane and he compels even his opponents to respect him & think well of him. Yes, that is the great thing; and both Dubois and Lansbury had it. And for the sake of the young ardent people there, who are always quickest to grasp that sort of thing, I was so glad they were there.

BRANCHVILLE, January 1, 1914

The opera last night was a glorious success. After writing to you I went downstairs in the Seville & ate a sort of a dinner, & then went down to the dingy & smelly Thalia Theatre. The usual audience was there. I tried hard to think of some one whom I might get to go with me, but did not succeed and went alone. There was not much that was attractive until the curtain went up. People wandered about the floor,—some of the men with their hats on, as I dare say you may already have seen them doing in some little Italian theatre, if you have happened to look in at any of the places where the people go. Italian audiences are much more free & unceremonious than ours,—which leads us to say they have

---

[18] William Edward Dubois, editor and author.

bad public manners. The conductor looked like d'Ascoli, and gave a very good account of himself, though I preferred the one we heard in Harlem. The same tenor sung, & gave an even better impersonation than we heard him give. He had considerable help from the girl who sang Violetta. She was very dramatic and powerful & sang well, though it was hard for me to believe she was Italian. She pronounced her words with quite an English intonation at times. But the play as a whole got the result that they always aim for. One forgot all about the surroundings and became passionately wrapped up in the progress of the thing. It got tears out of me by the hatfull, and for the time being I was as much in the play as anyone on the stage. I think this is what makes success in opera. The audience was very enthusiastic & uproarious, and so it was all carried along bravely. I was surprised to see that the properties were uncommonly good and the costumes really splendid. Usually these things don't get much attention.

There was an enormous crowd on the streets, but except for some racket at midnight, it was quieter than heretofore. The papers described quite elaborate doings at the hotels, especially in the way of dancing. But I saw nothing of it,—only a number of plain and fancy drunks, as samples of what I presume was a very large miscellaneous line that the city had on exhibition during the night. Well, that way of entertaining oneself no doubt has its interest for those who like it.

I think I have my speech pretty well in hand for the 7th, only I wish I could think up a few stories or bits of humour to lighten it up with. It ought to do pretty well,—I will speak without notes—yet I always have to get along without the assistance of any rhetoric in my speeches, merely telling a straight story & stopping when I am through. These women I am to talk to are influential & much in earnest, and I am going to make a point of warning them against over-confidence in direct political action, and get in some other matters that they do not usually hear. I believe it would be most useful, practically, if I told them that equality will not be so well served by their working their brains in behalf of

social legislation as by their coming among the unprivi-
leged & teaching them to hate their poverty & misery
instead of acquiescing in it; and at the same time, teaching their own friends & families to hate their wealth
that has come to them out of privilege, instead of acquiescing in it. I dare say that with luck I can manage
very well, and perhaps get a proportion of them with me.

But my writing is a sad and discouraging mess. I
can do nothing more with editorials,—that is certain—
and these other things I am on are no credit to me, and
worked out with unaccountable dryness & difficulty.
I'm glad I got my few words about Mawruss's book off
my hands before this general collapse set in, whatever
it is. Probably I'll pick up & go on again, soon, in a
satisfactory way; but I had misgivings about this winter & what I would be able to accomplish in it,—and
it seems as though, for no special reason, apparently,
they might have some foundation. I am sorry, for I
never had so many or so good opportunities; but one
can only try, after all. One isn't responsible for success
or failure, but only for the effort; and I am making
that to the best of my ability. Now I must go to bed
and see what the sand-man wants of me.

NEW YORK, January 6, 1914

At eight o'clock I leave for Pittsburg, where I appear
in all my warpaint and feathers next day. Thursday
I spend in a place called Erie, tinkering with a special-
ist, to find out what the devil ails my throat or neck or
something down that way,—not much, I know, and if
I were free, white & twenty-one, I'd let it go till it got
ready to behave itself as most things do if one only has
sense enough to let them alone & think about something else. But since I am in the hands of my friends,
at present in foreign parts, I feel it is part of my duty
to go and be pawed over by a solemn old grafter who
will tell me I have serious symptoms of everything from
the blind-staggers to the dry rot. Present company always excepted, what an ass anybody is to have any more

to do with doctors than to play poker with them once in a while in a friendly way.

Rutger Jewett[19] gave me a very nice lunch & some pleasant conversation at the Hoffman House instead of the Players Club yesterday. He told me Mawruss's appointment to Belgium was confirmed,—but he had heard nothing from him, any more than I have. I suppose he will be sailing soon, but it isn't likely I will see him again. I hope he will have courage to rise above his circumstances and do something beside loaf over there, but I doubt if he will. You must call & see him on your way home, if you go up that way.

From Erie I go on to Detroit & from there to Calumet, where the worm dieth not & the firewater is not quenched. I will come down by way of Chicago and return here promptly.

For my part, ever since I have been keeping close to the situation in the Calumet Mines which are owned almost entirely in Boston, I have been driven into such a vindictive hatred of New England that if you ever get me within gunshot of the South County again, it will be because I'm tied & carried there. I'm going to write Washburn and D. & what few friends I have up that way that they must wash up & disinfect before they seek my gracious society hereafter. It passes my comprehension how a girl of your instincts could endure a life of thirty years among people whose utter cruelty and thrice-damned inhumanity surpass anything I ever heard of in the South Sea Islands. The only comfort I have at this moment is in remembering that a long-suffering God will some day close three fingers and a thumb around the region and shake those cold-nosed Brahmins into the lowest depths of hell as a thrifty housewife shakes cockroaches into the fire off an unused dishtowel. And while he doesn't need any help on his job, if he ever advertised for volunteers, I'd be willing to spend a good share of eternity down there with a pitchfork, poking them back if any of them got his

---

[19] Editor with D. Appleton Company, then with Appleton-Century Company.

hands on the rim of the kettle. Fine charitable thoughts I'm indulging in. Maybe I'll be sorry for them some day, but at present, after the press reports of Calumet, my charity peters out at New England people and their first cousins, the copperhead snake. Never again do I want to see the South County,—I don't want to be so close when the crash comes.

You are missing a lot by being out of the country this winter. Congress is in a ferment of radicalism. It is a joyful sign that no machine can control its members. The political machine can't control Congressmen any more, even under the Wilson régime. Labour is breaking away from its leaders & taking the bit in its teeth. A labour leader has to run like a scared dog to keep ahead of the mass of his followers. The Morgan firm has voluntarily resigned from twenty-seven of its directorates. This morning's paper says the Ford automobile company has inaugurated a real profit sharing plan, dividing ten million dollars this year (1914) among its 23,000 employés,—an eight hour day, a minimum daily wage of $5, and no employé can be discharged save for unfaithfulness or hopeless incompetence. They say they do this under conviction that labour is not getting its share of the returns. It's a big year. How far back in the dark ages all this makes Carnegie seem,—Mark Hanna & the rest, whose word we used to take as law.

Well, I have gossipped long enough. Now I must start off & get my berth on a sleeper, & then throw together a few more ideas for a speech as the evening wears along.

DETROIT, January 9, 1914

I won't have to say a word in public all this trip, unless the Transportation Club finds out I am here to-morrow. I don't believe there will be anybody up in Calumet for me to address. One can keep busy enough dodging bullets without risking a harangue to the striking miners—poor souls. My heart has been pretty full of that, but I have tried not to write much about it to you. Bishop Williams the other day, said that when the New England mine owners made 1600 per cent profit year after year & created no better living conditions than existed in the mine regions, it made us wonder whether it was a good thing to hand over our natural resources to private development. I should think so. Every night for a month I have gone to bed with the pious wish that I could kidnap you, telegraph D. and A. to stand from under, and then start in at the head of 250,000 men and clean that whole abominable region up like Attila in Italy or St. Patrick in Ireland. But then I always remember how much better a job the Lord will make of it some day than I would, and so I am satisfied to wait.

Now I think I will walk around the hotel lobby a bit and then turn in. Poor old Mawruss hasn't written me since his appointment was confirmed, so I suppose he is going. We talked about it while I was there, but I didn't attempt to dissuade him because I saw his conscience was very uneasy, & thought it would make a better job of it in the long-run. Well, whisky isn't the worst temptation or addiction in the world after all, nor does it make the worst wrecks,—& I'm not very fond of whisky either.

CHICAGO, ILLINOIS, January 15, 1914

I have been here these past two days, and take the train at 10:30 tonight to go up on the Copper Range. I will get to Houghton at 11 tomorrow morning. Again I haven't written to you because I have been in such an unamiable frame of mind. In Detroit I had to listen, for instance, to very sharp criticism of Henry Ford, and it drove me into an awful state of indignation. Ford is wholly ignorant of economics & everything else but mechanics. He simply has blundered into a true conviction that his workmen are entitled to a division of what they earn. He clearly says he is not *giving* them anything,—what they get *belongs* to them, and he has no right to keep it from them because it is in his power to do so. The hopeless incapacity of his fellow-manufacturers to understand this simple idea has stirred me up to the boiling point.

And then these fearful things that are happening up in the copper country make the contrast terrible. The mines are owned chiefly in New England, and the owners exercise as absolute rights as any feudalistic power of the Middle Ages. There is at present no such thing as constitutional rights in the copper country. There is no law except the will of the mine owners. Men are shot and imprisoned and deported, and miners can work only on terms that it would be wholly repugnant to an American citizen to accept. I won't go into details,— probably you have read more or less about them.

Meanwhile, the owners are living agreeably in New England, and they are kind people, very generous & philanthropic. As Tolstoy says, they will do anything in the world for the poor except to get down off their backs. I have thought a thousand times of the friends that Tolstoy went among to get help in relieving the poor of Moscow. That picture,—perhaps you remember it—in the early chapters of *What is to be Done,* is one that will never die, it seems to me.

But I can hold myself down to decent reasonableness now, I think, and be in fairly good shape to meet you when you come back,—if the miners don't shoot me by mistake up on the Copper Range & I swear I wouldn't blame them if they did. I write all this just so you can see what I've been thinking about.

CALUMET, MICH., January 17, 1914

I awoke yesterday morning in the midst of this frightful country, and traversed it all the morning through one of the worst snow blizzards you ever saw, reaching Houghton at 12:30 noon. Making myself known, I soon got in the swing of things—got my general bearings and presently saw I had the foundation of a first-class story. I tramped all over the Quincy mine property which is on the heights opposite Houghton, and enjoyed a wonderful and impressive winter view such as I have seldom seen.

While the weather is severe, I notice the same physical exhilaration that I used to experience up in Canada. Last night, for instance, I slept just as I did in Winnepeg, a very light sleep, in which I seemed to be conscious of everything, but which rested me thoroughly.

Last evening I went to a hockey game, the first I had ever seen, & I found it tremendously exciting. There are great possibilities of personal injury in the game. It is the high-class local sport in this region.

This morning I came to Calumet & have been all over the mining property and the three villages and found out everything I want to know. I have a tremendously good story, I think, and one that every other writer has missed,—and it is the real story. How they could all have missed it, I don't see.

Conditions of labour have been shockingly misrepresented. I have just read a newspaper letter in the Chicago *Examiner* by our old friend Russell, which is the worst ever. There is plenty to say about the situation, giving everybody full credit all round, without telling such horrid falsehoods.

I am going back to Houghton now, and tomorrow being Sunday, I will spend the day among the strikers and Federation people over in Hancock, and go down to Chicago on the night train. I got all I want here in a surprisingly short time and want to go homewards.

The townspeople are a fine set. It seems strange to be at this club, where everything is so comfortable & up to date, and realize that one is out on the end of Keeweenaw Point that sticks up into Lake Superior, far and away out of the world. I had lunch here with the Calumet & Hecla mine manager & a couple of prominent citizens, and the Manhattan Club could hardly do any better.

CHICAGO, January 18, 1914
Monday morning, 11:30

I thought I had better hurry up & tell you that I got out of the copper country without being assassinated or having to confront any particularly murderous savages or, indeed, anything worse than a perfectly wretched night on the sleeper. Both sides to this dreadful controversy treated me as well as one could possibly be treated, and I saw no distress or violence except one little mess on a streetcar I was on, & that didn't amount to anything at all.

When I went up, the general manager of the Calumet and Hecla was on the car,—in fact, he & his bodyguard were the only passengers beside myself. If I had been in his place I would rather have taken chances on the strikers than on the bodyguard, for he was about as hard looking a character as I ever laid eyes on in my life. Dynamiting trains has been one bright particular feature of the general enterprise up there.

I see by the paper that poor old Mawruss has gotten under way towards Belgium. He may have written me, but I rather doubt it, and I haven't written him. I suppose he couldn't resist the inducement. Curious effect of public life,—when a man once has had his feet in the trough, it seems he never has the gumption to pull them out again, and in the longrun he never amounts to much. John Hay was as good an example as I know of. I wouldn't go through what Mawruss did when I last saw him, for a good deal. Well, when I saw he was pretty well set on going, I advised him to go, but I was disappointed—and sorry above all that the good old firm of Abe and Mawruss had to be dissolved, as I suppose it has. He may resign & come home, but I wish he had only had the clear sight & level head to stay home & produce some work such as he might.

I got a great story up in the copper country, a story of simon-pure feudalism. There is no public property in Calumet. The company owns even the ground that the streets are laid out on, that the schools & churches & public halls are built on. The whole thing is a benevolent despotism. I won't go into particulars, but I think I can make a very good story of it & one that will compel anyone who reads it to do a little thinking, at any rate.

But the sojourn on the sleeper was certainly bad, and I feel a lot like a boiled owl today. I am getting superb

results from the Metchnikoff treatment, gaining flesh &
looking husky. I must weigh myself presently for general results. But my throat aches & bothers me, & I
had expected to be wholly rid of that nuisance by this
time.

NEW YORK, January 27, 1914

My throat seems a good deal better this morning,
which is a pleasure. It has had a way of feeling better
& then going back; but I'm quite sure there is no serious trouble with it, and I'm glad I didn't bother with
doctors. They would probably have flourished around
in there with knives and scissors until they had my
whole talking apparatus out in a glass jar. If I had to
lose any faculty, I would as soon it might be speech as
any other, and far rather lose that than either hearing
or sight; but I don't propose to lose any of them without knowing the reason why.

Of course I can't tell anything about my plans until
after I have been to the office. I would really like to
give up going to the South and West, in spite of all the
interest of the trip and the real chance to do something
for the single tax. Maybe my keenness will revive, and
perhaps something of great special interest will break
loose by the middle of next week. You can never tell.
But my inclination at present is to stay tight at home.

When I look out at this weather and the rather commonplace sights, I realize what a lucky gal you are to
be in Italy. I couldn't be selfish enough to envy you,
and yet

> "I donta care what else you do
> So long you donta sent to me
> No posta-card from Napoli."

But there is lots of interest in living here this winter,
and really I have seen some very stirring things happen,
—and no doubt I am more useful and better off than
I would be in sunny It.'—only it's mighty pleasant there,
which is more than you can say for this.

I'm afraid I may have to spend a couple of days in Boston next month, so you will probably hear me sputter a good deal. Shaw & I will doubtless spend that much time with Dean Gay. I won't have to mix among the Brahmins, but I have cultivated such a dislike for them, I am sorry to say that the whole region is utterly hateful to me. If I were called on to point out the very worst gang of people in the world, I'd pick the New England capitalist, for evermore. But I reckon I'll live through a couple of days there without murdering anybody, though I know I'll feel like it from the moment I arrive until I leave.

Now I'll jump for one more train. It will be nice to see my mother, & count up the dog & the cats & chickens. I am looking out at the people going by on 34th St., & they look pretty haggard,—not a bit like the folks you are looking at. Don't forget to think about me once in a while, for I'll bet I feel a lot more like an exile right here in New York than you do in Italy. "Solo, profugo, rejetto," as Lionello sings, in *Martha*. The Chicago opera season closes with *Martha* this week. Glad I'm not hearing it, but I wouldn't probably have had the grit to stay away. After all, men are pretty weak sisters. Aint it? "The stronger sex" always made me smile. We are not, unfortunately. We are the more logical & conscientious, but not the stronger.

CAMBRIDGE, March 25, 1914

Tomorrow I see Sedgwick at noon and make some kind of appointment with old Charles William Eliot.[20] Pretty fine old chap, that,—eighty years old last Friday. I suppose I will have some amusement out of Sedgwick, & I will write you whatever is especially worth noting.

Hanging around here is getting to be a bit of a bore. I used to make my home in college circles,—& not so many years ago, at that—but I can realize now how quickly I would pine and wither if I went back to such

---

[20] President of Harvard, 1869-1909.

a life. I was never really meant for it; though I was very contented for a long time & can quite see myself over again in the attitudes & ideals of some I meet here now. It all seems very strange. I only hope I can pull up & get loose at the end of this week or at least by Monday. It will distress me abominably if I am not.

SCRANTON, Pa., April 23, 1914

[We] have been counting up the few remaining relatives and friends, and noting the changes in the city. My mother's home was here, when she was a young girl. Seeing the old bits of furniture—pictures, books & ornaments—brings back a great many incidents of childhood that had passed out of my memory, & make me realize how far I have gotten away from the things they represent. There was a very substantial quality about the family life of those days, and I tried to do it justice in my Gary article that Sedgwick has, but I am more & more convinced that the effort to reproduce it is vain. The circumstances that produced it exist no longer —at least, for the great majority of us; and the attempt to make it to order, as you may say, results only in a palpable imitation. Each generation, I reckon, must fix up its own institutions out of the material that the good Lord assigns to it, and not try to fit its life into the frame that was architected by another age,—quite as each oyster has to secrete its own shell. It's a very considerable job and a prayerful one, but we must do it, I guess, or fall by the wayside.

I am glad above all things of your success and interest in the job you have tackled. It makes one feel a great deal easier & happier; and looking over my knowledge of you in the past four years, it seems delightful that you have found yourself so splendidly. It is good too that you are with people who realize so well that no institution can be placed above the man or the woman, —that what you do for the Peoples Institute is only incidental & that the great thing is what it will do for you. And you will find that it will do a great deal,—

that the contacts you make & the insight you get will be very valuable. Presently you will find you have a great deal to give out to the world, and when that time comes, the opportunity & the mode of expression will come naturally along with it. So you can be very quiet, confident, observant, retentive,—you are well started, & need only let everything have its chance to happen in an orderly way.

Now I'll turn in, and see you Monday at the Brevoort at one o'clock.

CHICAGO, May 14, 1914

I left Urbana at seven o'clock & just reached here, and for some foolish reason dropped in at this old hotel to spend the night rather than go on to the University Club. To tell the truth, I think I wanted the welcome I was sure of, instead of being immersed in the gloomy though magnificent surroundings up there where I would be reminded at once of last winter and Calumet, and could see myself sitting at the desk in the library, writing one of the miserable letters I used to afflict you with. I haven't felt so very cheerful today, and am very glad indeed that I am on the last lap of my journey. I don't know whether I can get away again by Sunday or not but I shall try to, and the next you hear of me will be from Erie. I am going to try a little line of treatment of my own on that throat between now and then, nothing that can hurt it and may do me good. It was meaner than a strange dog this morning but rather took a turn at behaving better later in the day.

Well, that fine fellow[21] was delighted to see me and we had a good visit. What a solid comfort he is,—always solidly there when you put your finger on him and never disappoints one. I had never seen his wife before & found her a very nice, bright girl and natural, unaffected & likeable. They both took me in with a deal of affection, and we had long and satisfactory talks. He sails

---

[21] Clarence Boyer, a friend from his days in Titusville, Pennsylvania; Boyer was on the faculty of the University of Illinois.

for Europe next month and needs the change for he is worked down a good deal. I had a delightful night's sleep, & saw the University of Illinois, quite an impressive place, full to overflowing with the children of the prairies: boys with brilliant rosy cheeks & big home-grown girls right off the farms. It gives one an idea of the immenseness and diversity of this country as one wonders what place will be found for all of them. The whole region gives the impression of vast fertility. Everything takes its tone from the soil and inspires one with a sense of the beauty & delight of production. There is the enormous contentment of being close to the earth. Perhaps one would be a little restless & circumscribed there, but in spite of the rather low order of intelligence, there is a good deal coming out in the expression of their faces that one is bound to envy for a day or two, anyway.

But seeing them enables one to understand so many things. Methodism and revivalist religion—Prohibition—such things as these are the natural expression of their grotesque & half-comprehended emotional life. Party politics are the extent of their vision and a narrow un-amiable social life is the limit of their capacity. You can understand how they are led like sheep by Billy Sunday and fall into line behind Joe Cannon.[22] A day down there throws one back into the attitude of un-ending patience and consciousness of one's own limitations, and of the vast number of bungling and imperfect agencies by which good is accomplished in the world. So I have been thinking over some passages from Marcus Aurelius and feeling very thankful that everyone who tries to help people & encourage them isn't like me, and doesn't set about it my way. It makes me wonder afresh at the curious point of view of the reformer who wants us all to be alike or assumes that we are all alike. One wonders where he could have spent his days. And yet really, I suppose, many of us, reformers & all, spend our days wholly among our own kind with our eyes shut

---

[22] Sunday, a famous revivalist; Cannon, Speaker of the House of Representatives of the Fifty-eighth, Fifty-ninth and Sixtieth Congresses.

to the existence of any other. They do that at Newport and do it in Central Illinois, and maybe the Socialists and I.W.W.'s do the same. I wonder if I do, habitually.

CAFÉ LAFAYETTE, NEW YORK
Sunday, August 2, 1914, 11:10 A.M.

This is the one day and the time of day when it is a rare pleasure to be in New York. I had a good night, did not get up in a hurry, and about ten o'clock wandered down through Madison Square & Broadway to get a cup of coffee and two rolls, and write you this little line. I sneezed some, and am conscious that I have a nose, but I don't think I'll have a bit of serious trouble.

There was scarcely a soul stirring on the streets this morning, and it was strange to look down University Place from 17th St. as far as the eye could reach, and not see a single vehicle. It is just the genial bright warm weather that we had two years ago, & not a bit of stinging heat. It feels mighty good. This afternoon I shall simply walk around aimlessly, and wind up at Coney Island, for the evening. I am only staying in town to-day as a kind of antidote for the Pier;[23] and I am really enjoying it as never before. I feel I have been away so long that I am like a limbernecked stranger,—really I couldn't feel any more strange if I had been away five years. But all the disagreeable features of the Pier have already slipped out of memory, leaving the happy ones. Isn't it a mercy that it is always so?

The *Times* is worth looking at this morning, especially the editorial page. What a sad silly performance the war is; but men are so slow & weak about *thinking* that it may be the only means of awaking them to the necessity of pulling down the old idea of *government* and setting up the new idea of *administration*. The worst of the sentiment miscalled *patriotism* is that it obscures the difference between these two ideas and hinders the change.

I suppose poor Mawruss is distracted and busy as a

---

[23] Narragansett Pier, Rhode Island.

boy spearing snakes. You can bet that Minnie is the whole American legation at this crisis.

[Aug. 3, 1914]
Later, BRANCHVILLE.

Here I am—the country *so* beautiful, the weather *so* exquisite: the South County doesn't do itself proud at all by comparison (a-CHOO-OO-OO!!!). I looked out from the train-window coming in & there was my mother in a sweet clean little white frock waving to me; & I got up to the house in no time, kissed my mother, pinched both of Ethel's cheeks, looked over the dog & cats & the new chickens, had a supper & a lot of talk & here I am.

This country has a great opportunity and I firmly believe will accept it. If this war goes through to the bitter end it will have two effects over there. It will change the temper of the Continent by procuring for the people the idea of an ultimate personal judgment on all public matters. This is now one of the greatest differences between us and them. Over there, whatever the government says "goes"; here it doesn't go until we have looked it over. The second thing will be the putting down of the idea of *government* in favour of the idea of *administration,*—the difference between the Tammany idea in cities, for instance, as compared with the commission or business-manager idea. I don't think these changes can be long withheld after this war is over; and they will be a great blessing, for with them we can have a reasonable outlook for universal peace & without them we never can. If Carnegie had known how to spend money as well as make it, he would have spent some to further these ideas. Isn't it strange that a man who knows how to make money always assumes that he also knows how to spend it?—and what a mess they make of it, as a rule.

BRANCHVILLE, August 5, 1914

I got up this morning after a fair-to-middling night, blue as indigo—real weepy blues. I told my mother as Potash says in the play that if she said a single word to me I would go over in the corner and cry. Then I buckled down to the Auto[24] & got some good work done; and when I went to the postoffice after lunch and found your letter from Saunderstown telling what you had done, it turned all my feelings upside down in an instant & all the rest of the day I felt happy as a clam. Wasn't that a curious performance?

The Auto went very well today, but dear me, I am getting in awfully deep on this subject of law and government. Of course I want to say all I have to say, but it spins out so. I want to be brief and graphic and forcible, if I can; and I guess the only way is to go ahead and write and then go over it relentlessly afterward with the blue pencil and the scissors and cut and reshape the whole thing at once. I thought all this part was going to be very easy writing, but it is far from that. Still, I am so much encouraged with what you and A. Boyden think of the first part that I'm very enthusiastic over it and want to keep on. If I have luck, I will finish this section this week and then you may see how you like it.

Germany appears to be acting the part of absolute insanity. Now that the thing is started, I hope it will end by her being disintegrated & swallowed up. She has been the factor that has held modern Europe's progress back for forty years. By all means read H. G. Wells's message to this morning's *Times*.

Now I think I'll resist temptation to look over the Auto again, & go to bed.

The same good old South County weather is right here on the job. The air is like a cotton-wool blanket a mile thick. But the hay fever is on its last legs and a lot better today. My mother says I look like a June

---

[24] An autobiography that was never written. The Preface to the *Memoirs of a Superfluous Man* starts (p. iii) with the words: "It has several times been suggested to me, always to my great annoyance, that I should write an autobiography."

shad,—and I reckon from what the scales say and the way I feel, the Pier did peel me down pretty close. But I'd like mightily to go over the South County links again tomorrow, just the same.

CAFÉ LAFAYETTE, NEW YORK,
Sunday afternoon, August 9, 1914

I was struck with great sadness at coming here and finding nearly all our French waiters gone to the war & their places taken by Italians & Swiss strangers. I suppose I ought to feel worse that my dear old partner Mawruss is over there in the thick of it. But somehow there is not half the pathos about that that there is about these poor young fellows who are taken away from the most favourable opportunity of their lives, in industry & usefulness, and sent into a senseless work of devastation. But perhaps they do not feel it,—nature has queer compensations, & no doubt many of them are greatly elated.

I try not to accept anything the papers say, but if their reports are one-tenth part true, the Germans show a spirit like savages. What I look for is an uprising of the German people and a repetition there of what happened in France in 1870. But I am utterly out of heart at the thought that such simple & natural progress must come by such frightful means, when all that is necessary is to think clearly and proceed simply & logically, without selfishness & without hatred.

You are wrong about Battle Creek. Northern Ohio & lower Michigan were settled by an overflow from New England in the so-called Western Reserve. And as often happens, the emigration went into a state of arrested development, particularly in Michigan,—as the city of Victoria, British Columbia, for instance, is today more typically English than London. So for the peculiar social ideas & habits you mention, Battle Creek has backed Dedham or Providence right off the map. I never saw anything to compare with the isolation of those inland Michigan communities. I hope the Lord in his wisdom

& loving-kindness will see to it that I don't have to lay eyes on one again.

I still sneeze a little and feel somewhat dragged-out, but my spirits are as good as they can be in the face of this awful catastrophe, and I am accepting that with what philosophy I can muster, for the sake of the good that will certainly come. I am sorry Auto breaks off just at the interesting point where I gathered up my impressions & analyze them. But I'll have the rest for you shortly, I hope.

I think maybe I will go down to Coney Island again & get a breeze.

CAFÉ LAFAYETTE, NEW YORK,
September 4, 1914

I got a seat at Kingston. The ride down was extremely comfortable owing to a sudden fall in temperature that has produced a most delicious coolness here. I went to the Brevoort for the night, picked up your little letter & then came over here for dinner. I had clams, a slice of lamb, spaghetti and a chocolate eclair for dessert. Now I am in the café with a demi-tasse and one of them cigarettels.

My last few minutes with you straightened me out greatly. What a thing it is to feel that I have your splendid old clear head to fall back on when mine is a bit muddled & uncertain. I don't know whether I could do much in the way of good fiction, but one can anyhow try, and even if one fails, the effort is not wholly lost. You could help me on the dramatic side of it very much, & in fact you would have to buckle down & help wherever you could, or I wouldn't play. I think if I could cut my connection and give up all my responsibilities, & from now on indefinitely, set myself to writing only, it would perhaps be the most useful thing I could do. It wouldn't exactly be like starting all over again, or making my way afresh, since I have done more or less writing always, & am reasonably well known to publishers & editors.

So from now on I won't take on anything more, but devote myself to getting out of what I have. Chicago is pretty near self-supporting and gives me very little trouble; and I won't get drawn in any deeper there. I want to arrange for reporting on the single-tax as soon as possible, so that I can cover the ground for it no later than next spring. I want to write various aspects of it for two or three publications, if possible. The Outlook is already fixed up, and I think I'll try to add Colliers to the list. That with the American will make two weeklies & a monthly; which ought to give the subject a good airing. On the same trip I will pick up a couple of other articles,—I want to write one on the Doukhobors & one on the New Orleans opera. And if I see any others, I'll pick them up, and call that my last reporting trip for a good long time. It's something I could always go back to, I think, in case my other experiments in writing don't turn out as serviceably as they ought to. There's no use carrying anything "to the sweating point" as Marcus Aurelius says; and if the Lord wants me to keep on reporting, I'll find it out,—editing, too. But I've been thinking that the gradual changes which you & I have noticed both in the magazine & me, are a kind of intimation that maybe he has gotten me shaped around for some other sort of job.

You asked me what I thought of setting up parks & playgrounds in a city by private gift. They should be municipal institutions in a complete sense,—a public investment that the city puts its money into because it is very much worth while to do so. Our theory of municipal life is changing very much and at present it is in an anomalous condition. I think every private gift of this kind tends to blunt the city's sense of duty & corrupt its self-respect. I would never give a city a dollar's worth of anything as long as it continued to squander its social values by bestowing legal privilege,—franchise-values, land-values, &c.—which enable a large parasitic class to live without working and despoil the people of proper municipal institutions. I always thought Carnegie's gifts were vicious on this account.

BRANCHVILLE, September 9, 1914

This is another perfectly glorious day. I've got to go over to West Orange now and I haven't time to do more than scratch off a line to enclose you an editorial from last night's *Sun* that gives the best idea of the war situation of anything I have read. From all present accounts it seems that the Germans guessed wrong, from the start to finish and are in for a terrific whaling before they are through. I hope so, for I can't see anything else to end the rule of militarism in Europe. I wish it might be carried through to a finish, now that it is well started, and Germany completely disarmed before any intervention or mediation takes place.

Later, Wednesday night.

It looks as though Germany had really put its hand in the wasp's nest; and the attitude of this country & its press remains something to be proud of. We are re-opening the *Interpreter* in November; but I doubt your being much interested in it. The one for December you will like much better. I am thinking of writing an open letter to the Czar, and publishing it in the North American Review or the Atlantic. He will be the big figure after this war & we might as well get some public opinion focussed on him. It is rather a fanciful idea, but it might attract some attention.

Now I'll stop & visit awhile with my mother & maybe play a few tunes.

NEW YORK, Thursday, September 17, 1914

I must make my way up to the office now, and I don't look forward to it with any great pleasure. When I came in this morning I telephoned up, and feel as though somebody had kicked me hard in the pit of my stomach.

Let me tell you my troubles. Last week when I was over at Orange, I had the chance to write a little article about some of Edison's work, and in view of what we were talking about as the new standards of the magazine, I deliberately set out to write as badly as I could. In about two hours I had gotten off a complete success from that point of view. I read it over and "the ship rolled so" that I haven't been able to eat anything since. It was the most insincere, slipshod, exaggerated, meretricious thing that has been written in this city, outside of Hearst's office.

I mailed it in, expecting it would go in the wastebasket. I telephoned in this morning & found they were greatly pleased, had mailed the thing over to Orange & Edison O.K.'d it, & they are rushing it into print.

Such a thing seems incredible. I told them if they put my name to it I would sue them for slander; so there is the satisfaction that no one will know who wrote it. But it makes me awfully blue. I shall ask you to read a galley of it & see whether I am "hipped" in any degree, for I may be.

All this is part of the mad passion for size and popularity. I don't think I had better say any more about it, nor you either, until we see whether I'm right or wrong; but at present I feel pretty bilious & out of sorts.

Hotel "de Zalm," The Hague,
HOLLAND, January 27, 1915

Well, it is as I've always said: the higher up you go in the scale of government officials, the more worthless they are. I spent the whole morning today between the American Minister (van Dyke) and the German minister (von Müller) in an effort to get on my way into Belgium; and when I got through I was no nearer Belgium than I was yesterday.

Van Dyke was wonderfully pleasant and courteous; he kept me chatting a considerable while, and finally gave me a note to the German Minister, who was affable and agreeable and no end of polite, but couldn't do anything for me because the matter wasn't in his jurisdiction. By that time it was half past twelve, and I threw over in disgust any further tinkering with the legations and did what I should have done in the first place,—namely, took the 2 o'clock train to Rotterdam, found the German Consul, and he fixed me up ship-shape in twenty minutes; and now all I have to do is to catch a train at eleven o'clock Saturday morning. And that's another thing: that lackadaisical first secretary of ours told me this morning I would have to go clear down to Maestricht at the very south point of Holland, & cross over to Brussels by automobile. The German consul told me to go through Antwerp and go all the way by train, as the trains were running.

The moral is, if you want a very agreeable good time, the diplomatic service is the place to look for it; but if you've got business to attend to, the consular service is your only hope. Here endeth the first lesson. It merely remains now to be seen whether the military authorities will take any stock in the pass that the consul gave me; but I think I am framed up strong enough to get in pretty nearly anywhere.

An old German came in the consul's office at Rotterdam, and a very nice lovable old chap he was. He began to talk to me, & after we had gone far enough for him to see that my German was really about as poor an article as I claimed it was, he began to speak English. He was very sore at the United States for her attitude on the question of trade,—the first thing he said to me being, "Well, you people are all down on Germany, aren't you?" I suppose it is quite as impossible for them to get our point of view as it is for us to get theirs. I wouldn't be surprised if I had had it pretty well in those two Interpreters—letters to the Czar. But what I really started out to say is that one remark of his would make a feminist out of anybody, I should think, who had a grain of gumption. After saying that the war would be a dead loss all round—really speaking very humanly and nicely—he said "the only good thing I see is that it will make women cheap, and they can't afford to be so extravagant as they are now."

There's a fine sentiment for you. Pass it along with my compliments as a good specimen of the conservative attitude. Here in Holland it is fine,—if a man's wife leaves him he can send the police after her and yank her off the train like a deserter from the army. They say the Dutch women are waking up, however, & I hope they are. Suffragette measures aren't very nice, but it's pretty good to be born over there, if you are a woman, after all.

I'll write you again before Saturday, of course, and after that I don't know what I can do. Whatever mail goes through England is all pawed over and probably would reach you some time next year, if at all. I wish I were en route through Holland going home instead of to Belgium.

LONDON, May 5, 1915

It was such a good thing for me to come over. I am so well, and enjoying so many things of tremendous interest. Really you have no idea of how differently everything looks when one is on the ground. For instance, reading the cables here makes one perfectly certain that everybody over home is in a boiling rage over the torpedoed tank-ship, & ready to go to war at a minute's notice; and yet I know if I were in New York I would see no evidence of it at all. It is just so here. There is no appreciable difference except for the darkened streets, and the enormous solidity of the English nation isn't even scratched or shaken; and when one is in New York one thinks that everybody here is living down cellar among the coal & the potatoes.

The trip has been a great thing for my health, no doubt about that. I feel like a lord; & I'm eating English meals with the best sort of results, too.

I mailed my cards with yours to the House of Commons yesterday. I don't know whether Johnnie is in attendance, but he ought to be, for there are important doings. If he is, I will no doubt hear from him very shortly, and will write you of course at once. Now I must send off a note to my mother, for I think there is a mail going soon.

LONDON, May 7, 1915

We had a corking thunderstorm last evening, which worried me a great deal more than the chance of Zeppelins. I have talked with several men from the front, and they all express the hope that Italy & Holland & the United States will stay hands off & let the thing be settled between the present combatants. As far as we are concerned, I don't believe they need to worry. If we came in, we would be playing straight into Germany's hand, first by helping them to square themselves with their own people, & second by stopping the supply of war material to the Allies, since in that case we would need all we produced for ourselves. I believe our government realizes this and will not be tempted in—for if we went to war we could do absolutely nothing.

I mailed my introduction to Mr. Sutherland day before yesterday, but so far I have not heard anything from him. Members of Parliament have business to attend to in these days, and that makes them hard to get at. Beside, time seems to be no particular object over here, anyway. The casual & languid ways of the English are a delightful study for one who is footloose & not in any special hurry about anything. But to the Americans such as I see around London, who have fish of some sort or other to fry, they are very maddening. I ran across one chap who is trying his best to get $50,000 worth of German dye stuffs out of hock, and the language he used would blister paint. Everything is going very well with me personally, so I can more or less enjoy it; but no doubt I will have some delays myself before I get through.

I dressed up and looked in at the Savoy the other evening to see my American friend Thompson who was seeking relaxation on the dancing-floor. I am glad I'm not stopping there. It seems to be alive with people of dubious sorts—my opinion is that most of them are here to get what they can out of an empire in distress—vultures, mostly, though some are undoubtedly good folks enough. I met a Russian woman from Réval, a little French woman who looks like Madame Récamier &

speaks no English, and a couple of countesses, one French & one English. I talked about half an hour with the group & then some instinct suggested that I had better move on. I wonder whether it pays to be as much like a woman as I am in my dependence on instincts & "hunches." Still, they always work out all right, so I don't see why not.

Well, one thing seems certain: that these people are going to carry on the war to a positive end; and I am sure I hope they do. The closer I am to the situation, the more certain I become that after these beginnings, it is the only possible outcome. You see, these nations have all more or less (and Germany wholly) permitted themselves to believe in the doctrine of force—so here is the inevitable & necessary result. We in the United States must more & more give ourselves over to a better way. If we can consistently stick to it in the face of all provocations, our example will count for more than any amount of education by slower & more indirect processes.

I am sending off this little line because I think there is a mail out tonight. I don't pay much attention to the outgoing mails, merely scribbling my letters and dropping them in the box.

LONDON, May 10, 1915

It was so good to get your letters, for I specially feared they had gone down on the poor old Lusitania; but it appears she carried only a few bags of mail and so probably I lost nothing. I am afraid that you are more or less alarmed & worried, but I hope not for I see no reason for it—on my account, I mean—yet I can understand how one must be shaken up & distressed by these revelations of German character & the evidence of what they are willing to do. There was an air raid at Southend yesterday, but it did not do any harm to speak of, and London does not appear to be in any great state of excitement.

I have been fairly busy with one thing and another

& have had a good insight into a number of situations. I am very glad that the Germans have pushed the logic of war as far as it will go. I think it will at last urgently raise the question of whether there is any such thing as civilized warfare; and from that question it is a short step to international peace.

I am interested to see that we are not expected to fight on account of the *Lusitania*. None of the English papers hint at it, as far as I have seen. The general impression is that we can be of more help by keeping out than by coming in; which is of course correct enough. I hope the people at home will realize it as clearly as we do here.

In spite of so much evidence to the contrary I can not help clinging to the idea that Germany can not fight much longer with the consent of their own people; and I find that I get the same impression from men who have been there lately. I may be wrong, but I believe they already see the impossibility of carrying the financial burden a great while longer, with no better prospect of success. Still, one never knows; but I hope it is so.

Undoubtedly, the English are the strangest people in the world—a most curious lot they are with their languid ways of meeting emergencies. I like them better now than I did in peace time, but even now, one does not get very close to them. They give the impression of enormous stability. I believe there is much more war talk in New York than there is in London. A season of Russian and French opera opens on the 20th, which I wish you were here for. They sing *Pique-Dame, Eugen Onegin* and *A Life for the Tsar* among others, & the cast is said to be good. Speaking of Russia reminds me —I met some high-life riff-raff the other night, among them a handsome big Russian called Mme. Lastowska, who claimed to be good friends with Prince Dolgorouky and Nikolai Nikolaevitch, who bosses the Russian army. We had a long talk in which she warmed up pretty strong about her country & people & I chimed in favourably, of course, & we got along first rate. When I went away, she held out her hand, but my Continental manners slipped their trolly and I didn't make any offer to kiss it. So she held up the side of her face to be kissed, and then kissed me on the left cheek. It was a very solemn sort of performance and mighty entertaining to the Americans who were in the group. Thompson said he thought I ought to declare a dividend. I don't know how it impressed the English people, but to tell the truth, I was a good deal rattled.

I see some amusing things. Yesterday morning an American with a lame foot came into the Savoy, fresh from paying his doctor's bill. The doctor charged him $75 for five visits, and the things he said about him were worth hearing. I laughed myself almost into hysterics and could scarcely get up, for all I felt a lot of sympathy for him.

Now I must go out and look up some people. Your Mr. Sutherland has not been heard from; he must be sick or loafing on his job, as I find these Englishmen mostly seem to do. They turn out at 10 A.M., quit for lunch at 11:45, come back at 3:30 & go out for tea at 5. They get a lot of work done somehow, but there is no knowing how it is done.

LONDON, Sunday, May 16, 1915

Yesterday morning a very pleasant Scotch gentleman came in to see me, who turned out to be Dr. Archibald, Mr. John Sutherland's physician, and an extremely nice man. He began without any preamble by saying, "I'm sorry to tell you poor Sutherland is jolly bad." It appears that he is lying in the National Liberal Club—and I know of old what a dismal caravansery that is, in spite of all its magnificence, for I too lived there at a dismal time in my life—and he is down with his lungs again, and as Dr. Archibald says, he is "jolly bad." He is not up to the crisis yet, and the doctor is a good deal worried. He wants Mr. S. to go to a nursing home, but he sticks to the club with Scotch persistence.

So much for the bad news; but you can count on me to do all I can. Now for myself, I had today a most heavenly & delightful experience in my first view of

English country & country life, in perfect surroundings & a perfect day for showing "green & cloudy England" at its very best. Mrs. Minturn Scott asked me down to her mother-in-law's at Shoreham in Kent—Sir Joseph Prestwick's place that passed to the elder Mrs. Scott, his niece. I have it in my heart to say a great deal—the view, the endless number of birds, the endless variety & beauty of flowers & trees—I know now why & how it is that the English are born knowing all about birds & flowers—but I haven't anything in my head that would give you the faintest idea of it. It was far more than an ordinary experience, because it threw light on so much that was already in my mind. I can understand so much now that is in the English nature-poets, that before this I understood only imperfectly—so much of Gray & Kingsley & Wordsworth and many others —even the old hymn: "Bright fields beyond the swelling flood Stand dressed in living green." Mrs. Minturn Scott, a great radical, but of the political Socialist type, wandered with me all afternoon, & we lay on a green hill top overlooking the village—so old & compact and picturesque—and let our philosophies of life flow forth for each other's benefit in the happiest possible way, without argument or either of us trying to put the other "under conviction," & as a result I found we were not very far apart. She could not understand my indifference to direct political action, but came to understand it easily enough, & I for my part came to understand her leaning towards it. So it was a beautiful conversation.

The other inmates of the place were Mrs. Scott, a lovely Scotchwoman of sixty-five or so, & three daughters of middle-age—one married, but separated from her husband. They were all perfectly charming to me—they are tremendously intelligent and have beautiful old school manners. I was immensely surprised & gratified with the way the splendid old Scotch lady took me in. She personally conducted me all over her garden—it was wonderful, but it doesn't take the shine out of Edgewood,[25] although the place is on three times the scale

---

[25] Edgewood Farm, the home of Ruth Robinson.

of size—and meanwhile she prattled about her family, the absent sons, the dead husband and the present daughters, in the sweetest & most candid artless way in the world. There was no ice to be broken nor any skin to penetrate; which seemed very remarkable & interesting. In all respects my visit was one of the lovely and permanent benefits of one's life.

It is midnight & I must square away for a busy day tomorrow.

LONDON, June 11, 1915

I haven't the least idea when I can come home, but I have sort of set the 26th as a possibility, though it is wretchedly uncertain. Things drag so; yet I am really doing a great deal in ways that show for something. I am trying to get a different impression of our people disseminated through influential sections of the press. They are all wrong about us & our attitude in this war, and are in for a big disappointment, I am afraid.

The study one makes of these people & their way of doing things is vastly interesting, & I might have been here five years & learned less about it than I have picked up in five weeks, just because I got the right start with the right people. They are the most extraordinary that ever were made in the world; but there is so much that is wonderful about them. I can tell you about the labour leaders, the pacifists, the Democratic Control people, & the people in power. I had dinner Saturday night with the proprietor of the *Nation* at his home. Sir George Gibb & his wife were there & invited me to their pretty home at Wimbledon next day. While there I had a talk with the editor of the *Economist,* & then Lady Gibb showed me the remains of an early British camp, where they resisted the Roman invasion. Well, the Romans invaded, & so did the Normans, & I dare say the idea was quite as terrible then as the idea of German invasion is now. Yet somehow England has managed to do rather well after all; & I could not help thinking that the present strife is as foolish as that early one is now seen to be. The thing is, to outgrow governments; the people, left to themselves, don't act that way. Do you know, I have gotten a very decent & unexpected hearing for a good deal of that doctrine in some influential quarters here? This war will show that there is something in it; especially when the labouring class begins to turn, as it surely will. Their position, now & hereafter, is simply impossible, & mark my words, they will revolt.

Dear old Bill Bryan, may the Lord bless him—I don't know how he looks when one is as close to him as you are, but at this distance he seems like a real statesman. He has set these people guessing, I can tell you; & his resignation has made a lot of pleasant visions vanish from their eyes. I'm for him on the face value of what he has done, & wrote him a letter to that effect.

I have had a couple of notes from Mawruss. I doubt if I see him; he is in a wretched position, poor fellow.

NEW YORK, August 24, 1915

Last night was such a terror. The noise & heat just were beyond endurance. Happily I had the forethought to buy a bottle of mosquito mixture & pour it all over the bed, so I wasn't eaten alive—or bitten at all—though I know there were above a hundred million in my room. But I feel pretty seedy this morning. Jewett came for dinner & suggested a publisher for the book; so I'm going to try it on him. The *Evening Mail* people got me for lunch—old Sam McClure[26] & his financial backer who seems a very fine scholarly fellow. Sam left early & left me to the backer, who put up the idea of going to Europe again very attractively, but I turned it down. He wanted me to go with some great big Wall St. man —he didn't say who, & I didn't ask—who is going over to make a study of the relation of the individual German to the State. I would get everywhere, even to the Kaiser himself. Well, if I didn't have any mothers or any special responsibilities it would be a glorious thing to do, on

---

[26] Editor and publisher, founder of *McClure's Magazine* and president of S. S. McClure Newspaper Corp.

the chance of a lifetime. But I turned it down. I made up my mind that I was through with that sort of thing & henceforth would stand here with my bass fiddle as long as my feet hold out.[27] The old instinct is pretty strong, though, I must say,—imagine how I would have jumped at such a chance in my old vagabond days. I could make mighty good money by it too, which wouldn't be a bad thing just now, especially as it would come in such an interesting way. But I think I'll just keep on hammering on the xylophone, and let some other fellow play the rest of the instruments. I can't play them all, & may as well make up my mind to it.

BRANCHVILLE, September 17, 1915

Well, I got home early & in good season, & my mother brisked around & cooked me a scrumptious dinner of Hamburg steak, succotash, raw tomato salad, beets & fine peaches for dessert. It tasted powerful good. It's nice to be high-life at the Brevoort this baking weather, but we do badly on food. Somehow between Fannie's oleomargerine & alum rolls & eggs that were laid in the year of the great crash, followed up by French *chef-d'oeuvres* and symphonies in sauce, y'understand, you feel a wide & cavernous hankering for grub. I use the word grub in its most unrestricted sense.

UNIVERSITY CLUB, CHICAGO,
November 15, 1915

Thank you so much for your little letter. I will certainly go over to the Chicago immigrant station and tell you all I can find out about it. I am settled down here at my old quarters in preference to the Union League, partly because I am used to it & partly because the Union League has too many counterparts of K. I find that

---

[27] This and the following references to musical instruments are based on an old song from *The Spring Maid*, "You Can't Play Every Instrument in the Band."

out here, quite as I supposed, the President's marriage
has done him a heap of harm. I had confirmatory hints
of it when I was in Washington. It isn't altogether a
matter of taste, you know. The theory is that this lady
is a thorough child of the dominant interests, and that
she is undermining uncle Woodrow's democracy; and
people have the same kind of exasperation with that
now that they used to when the French king would send
over some high-grade Jennie to work old Charles II, for
instance. I really don't blame them particularly. But
however that may be, the old man is going to have rocks
in his pathway, especially if William J. turns loose, as
I think he will. I see the New Republic had something
quite strong to say about his Manhattan Club speech,
and what they say about it out here wouldn't be fit to
repeat.

I wish Woodrow hadn't tried to carry water
on both shoulders at once. He wasn't built for a juggler.
But I am not worrying any. I still think if he had come
out strong for some real principles, it would prove to
be the best politics of all. Still, I suppose you can't
play every instrument in the orchestra,—you can't be a
philosophicker and a politicker at the same time. That
has always been a favourite theory of mine & I believe
'tis true.

I saw Thompson this morning & his first inquiry was
for you; so you made your customary big hard hit. If
I were going into the politics business & could take
you along, we would sweep the deck—but when the good
Lord stood us up on the carpet at the end of our course
& asked what we had been doing with our talents, we
might be sorry we hadn't stuck it out at the old stand
as philosophickers.

Now I run on.

On board S. S. Kristianiafjord
(Norwegian American Line)
July 25, 1916

This has been a great thing for me. I have made a

business of being as idle and lazy as possible, & now I feel wonderfully picked up & keen for my job. It has been a very uneventful trip & we have had perfect weather all the way, except for a dash of fog night before last when we were coming into Kirkwall. The passenger-list is made up of Norwegians principally, with a sprinkling of people of all sorts and kinds, trades & professions,—a Pole, a Siberian from Omsk, naturalized Austrians & Germans, and nearly everything else you can think of. Nearly all of them are interesting. I like the Norwegians very much; they are intelligent, affable & very dignified, and thoroughly democratic without stopping to bother about what the word means. I am greatly interested in their music & in their food. Our band has been playing marches & chorales that have come down from the Thirty Years War, & I tell you they are wonderful. Those people must have been fighting for a principle to produce such music. All the music that comes out of this war will be the chink of one silver dollar against another, I'm sorry to say.

Speaking of music, we have two or three opera fellers on board,—a basso from Munich, Miss Hempel and a Viennese soubrette who is very interesting and charming. Her husband is an actor in the Imperial Theatre at Vienna & is also interesting & charming. I have talked a great deal with them & it is surprising how my small stock of German comes back. Miss Hempel is quite pretty on the stage, but alas, at close range she is nothing but a frumpy squatty little German girl, not very intelligent but very pleasant & good-natured, and she does not seem to have any affectations. The curious thing is that she seems almost awkwardly diffident,— blushes when you speak to her & drops her eyes; one would suppose being so much before the public would have done away with that sort of thing.

I haven't written a word since I came on board, or done anything serious except talk a little about our plans; and it has been the best thing in the world for me. Our course lay very far north, and the long days are curious & fascinating. It seems so odd to see a good strong twilight at twelve o'clock—midnight. Some of the

Norwegians told me that they didn't sleep much in summer, for they did not feel the need of it. I suppose they make up for this in winter.

I shall be immensely interested in Scandinavia. I can see it coming. I have already noted how steady the companionship is between men & women. After lunch & dinner on board, all hands go up to the smoking room, for coffee & whatever else they want,—men & women, all together. The manager of the Christiania street railways is on board,—a very intelligent man,—& he told me that this perfectly free & easy companionship runs all through life in Norway. They study, work & play together. I shall see more of this and have it to tell you about when I return.

Poor sister Doty has seen enough on this trip to open her eyes if such a thing were possible. She goes around among these affable Norwegians dressed in a most curious way, & tells them that they ought to do away with their kings & change their form of government. I was very much interested yesterday when she declared herself against rich people & well-dressed people, to a very sensible Swede woman,—who told her quite naturally that such a point of view seemed extremely snobbish & exclusive, & for her part she thought it wasn't becoming to make oneself conspicuous in dress or otherwise. It seems incredible that a woman can travel about the world as much as she has without reducing her pride of opinion or modifying her whims and fancies. But apparently it can be done.

BRANCHVILLE, Tuesday night,
September 12, 1916

Tennis was nice. There was quite a crowd out on the courts this afternoon and I played about four sets. It went pretty well, for I didn't go in full strength by any means,—I didn't win anything, but didn't care about that for I was more interested in seeing how my ankle behaved and in sort of warming up and getting the range for tomorrow. Ankle held up quite nicely and I think by another day will be all right.

It is a delicious crisp night, & the crickets & katydids are all singing. It used to make me sort of blue, but my late experiences have gotten me bravely over that. When it got dark at seven o'clock tonight, I thought of Norway and I was the tickledest fellow you ever saw. It is very hard to understand how easily too much is enough, even of a good thing, until you have a good strong contrast given you; & then you wonder how you could ever be so foolish. I've changed a lot in a couple of years. Of course we don't know what might have been if the war hadn't come, but it did come & I seen enough already, so I am not at all keen any more about going over to end my days in France or sunny It. The Lafayette is enough like France to do me for a while, & Washington Square in summer is plenty like sunny It. So I maybe remain here to live & go abroad to visit. When I want to mix with Norwegians again, I'll take the subway to Brooklyn & if I need any more Italians than I can find around the Square, I'll take the Erie out to Paterson, N.J., and think how nice it is to live in a land where everybody isn't like everybody else, and where you can get 'most anything you want.

I feel well & happy tonight. My mother gave me a beefsteak for dinner,—isn't that extravagance for you in these times? One of our new kittens wandered into the dining-room & had to be drove out. He has come up into a fine long-legged cat, & is a great hunter,—he & his mother keep the premises clear of mice, & they are on their job day & night. The house is full of spiders—harmless ones, so we let them crawl around; & I killed a few flies this morning. I'm told there has been hardly any flies about, all summer, & we never have mosquitoes.

BRANCHVILLE, September 20, 1916

I have been setting my wits to work on problems of farm plumbing and concrete flooring all this beautiful day, the very best of autumn weather.[28] It seems a simple matter to carry a stream of water through a pipe to where it will do the most good, but somehow it doesn't turn out to be so simple when one gets down to doing it. Maybe you have heard of things like that.

Well, I wrote to George Creel,[29] & shall meet him at the Player's Club, give him my paper & find out if there is anything more that I can do. I also sent a line to Newton Baker, saying that I am here & available. It seems queer to be putting myself forward for service in a political campaign, but for the first moment in my life I really feel that politics does matter this time; I was going to start in on some profitable writing, but if my services can be used in the next six weeks for the good of the country, I'll postpone my money-making enterprises until after the election and call it a full summer in the public service. If nobody wants me to do anything, of course that will be the end of it; but I felt I ought to make the offer because I think it is really imperative that Mr. Wilson & his present crew, poor as they are, should keep on deck another four years. I think I can help a little, if they requisition me, and then after election, whichever way it goes, I shall forget all about it & go to work along the old lines. You will approve of that, I know.

I suppose that all they will want is writing, unless they ask me to speak to some academic audiences maybe. I don't care,—and particularly I don't care if they don't want me to do anything.

According to the papers, the strike prospects look rather bad again. It is almost inconceivable that the unions will call out all the allied trades & interests. If they do, the city will look rather flat on Friday, when I go in, and I may walk up to the Player's Club, which won't hurt me a bit; but the same condition that gives

---

[28] AJN's stays in Branchville were at the home of a cousin and her husband. The latter ran a farm. As far as I know AJN knew nothing about farming or anything connected with it. His contribution was probably that of a spectator.

[29] Editor and writer, chairman 1917-19 of Wilson's Committee on Public Information.

me a little good exercise will work no end of hardship for no end of people. I entirely agree with you in your sympathy with the men. They are so villainously led that I think they are to be sympathized with more when they are successful even than when they fail.

BRANCHVILLE, September 30, 1916

Quite as you prophesied, I've got a change of plans in prospect. There's rather a disappointment in it, too, or the prospect of one. You see, when I got home I found I had the urgent suggestion of some work in the city of Baltimore very much on the lines of the little job I did some time ago for the Mayor's Commission in Chicago, you remember, in regard to taxation. I shall take up the suggestion at once with a view to finding out more precisely what it means, and if it pays as well as the Chicago job did, of course I'll take it. The disappointment is that it won't leave me very much time to save the country by being a politicker, and I had quite set my heart on that. However, perhaps I can work in something at odd times; only I had rather 'lowed as how I would give up these six weeks to helping Woodrow. But if this turns out to be a good thing, I'll take up with it.

If my cold keeps on improving, I shall go down to Baltimore Sunday night and be home again Monday evening. They invited me down at their expense to talk it over; and of course I'll let you know immediately what I think about it and what I've made up my mind to do.

My cold keeps on getting better—the pain is out of my chest and I have my taste back. My mother is steaming up the croup-kettle at all hours & has me plastered with oil and camphor.

BALTIMORE, Monday,
October 9, 1916

I'm sure it was the weather; for with the first prospect of the fine cool breeze now blowing over us, I picked up & began to feel lively as a kitten & as though I were a real citizen & nothing could go wrong. But yesterday & last night I certainly had 'em: not ill, but blue, —blue as indigo. All over now; the air is fresh & strong and I am in first class fighting trim.

Well, that submarine must have been jumping around yesterday like a billion-dollar special, for it made a first-class clean-up. All the ships down here are tied fast to their docks, wondering what those enterprising enthusiasts are going to do next. As long as they play by the rules & don't sacrifice any lives, I am willing to recognize the element of humour in the situation. To drop in at Newport just long enough to mail a letter, & go out again without buying even a package of cigarettes is stepping high, wide & handsome, for a little submarine 3000 miles from home; and I confess to being just sport enough to be interested and willing to hand them all the munitions and war supplies that they can sink in the next six months. As long as they confine their aim to that class of freight, I am for them. But it is really laughable to think of a lot of Uncle Sam's destroyers standing around like spectators at a prize-fight, watching the little fellow clean them up. If I didn't have business to attend to, I'd go over to Washington & get Daniels to let me go out on one of those destroyers to watch the game.

But instead of that I must keep my head full of paving assessments, docks, schools, parks & such like, —and much the better for me I dare say. I don't know whether I can possibly get up this week or not, but I'll know later.

I think the funniest thing about this submarine affair is to think of our navy having to turn out & clean up after them. Our destroyers weren't built for the passenger trade, and I'll bet the commanders hate the job.

LOS ANGELES, May 5, 1917

I think I pretty well have the measure of Southern

California. Its contribution to civilization apparently consists in furnishing physical comfort at rather a cheap outlay of effort and money. That seems to be about all there is to it; and hence it attracts chiefly those persons who have dedicated their lives to comfort, and are more interested in comfort than in anything else.

I have been driving all the afternoon: I went down to Gardena where there was a sort of county fair going on a small scale, and I looked the people over very carefully. They do not look like the Utah farmers—far from it. Then I drove back through great orange groves and orchards & gardens of various kinds to Pasadena, & then along their show street—Orange Grove Avenue, isn't it?—where so many handsome residences are; and so home. Dr. Shiels took me—he had a schoolvisiting errand that did as an excuse for a long drive. He is quite keen on the natural beauty of the region & wanted me to see it.

I could tell instantly why you didn't warm up to life down here. In spite of all its comforts & beauty & cheapness & pleasant smells, it isn't *interesting*, it has nothing to satisfy any further demand. That is the great test, & this place doesn't fill the bill. New York does, with all its faults & so does Salt Lake. I hear San Francisco does, but I'll soon find out. I am working all this out in an article, and I shall mention the South County.

I now go up to San Francisco. I rather hate to spend all tomorrow on a train & think I shall manage some other way. What I'd like to do is to lie off a couple of days & finish the Salt Lake article that my head is so full of,—only it would put me back. So I'll move on and write in odd minutes as best I can.

To Ellery Sedgwick

July 14, 1917

DEAR SEDGWICK:

Thank you for your attention to my half-breed French friend's paper on the church and the saloon. If he does not succeed with it elsewhere I shall take it up again with you; and if you think better of it meanwhile, write to me.

I was depressed by your editorial note to the German-American press in the July issue. The article was indifferent enough but the note was discouraging. Fudge, Sedgwick,—fiddle-de-dee! It sounded like the anserine squeak of an old maid who sees a mouse. Don't you know there never was a day since the war, at least when I was there, that I couldn't buy the London papers at any stand in Berlin? It is only your precious Liberal friends who talk as you do about "the enemy language." You have taken up their parable. They are nothing but constitutional Tories at heart, and under stress of plain fear —sheer, besetting, craven dread—have hurriedly picked up a little vague patter about liberty and democracy, as a sick crook turns to prayer. I am sorry for them. It must be an awful thing to be the victim of such abject mental states. But I hate to see you go their way.

And then you propose a censorship. Can't you think of something new, and something that will work? That is the Puritan sequence,—scare him, and he turns instantly to the thought of force-majeure. And then, a tax on "the enemy language." Sedgwick, I don't like the German language, and I differ from many in thinking it has no literature that is much worth while; but one thing is certain,—it has been in use a good while and will be used long after you and I are gone. There is a good deal of it being spoken in the Kingdom of Heaven at this moment and if the blessed saints and the Apostles can stand listening to it, I don't know but what it is good enough for Boston. But aside from that, the point is that when the masters of your mind, those who manipulate you into this state of sickly dread for their own purposes, when they get their trade-routes fixed and the rest of their objects gained, then it won't be the enemy language any more. We shall always have to live with Germans, talk with them, find fault with them, admire them, take what they have to give us and let them take from us. There's no way out of that, so why not be a little more imaginative at present, and live a little more in the larger scope of things?

You see, for some reason that I don't quite understand, I have been always fond of you and in a way, proud—proud of your achievement and of the way you have made a place for liberal thought. I hate to see you get into such a ludicrous funk,—it's pitiful. Be on the side that is coming out ahead in the long-run; quit the short-time point of view. What makes nations great is the manner of spirit they are of; it is their Geist and their Ernst der ins ganze geht, if you won't tax me two cents apiece for those words before I get my fall crops in; and not their armies or censorships or suppressions and commandeerings, and especially not their fears. And how can the American nation have Geist unless you and I have it? It is trying to do without it that has made this mess; and how is the mess helped if you and I let go the little that we have?

Why not remember that we and our small doings are in the hands of a power that is strong enough to make it safe to seek the truth and good enough to make it right to tell the truth?—all without the need of being afraid of anything or anybody in particular. If the Lord's arm is shortened to the extent that we must tax haben sind gewesen gehabt worden sein's and censor the German press in order to be saved, we have a mighty blue prospect before us. You may smile at my old-fashioned notion, but if it came down to a choice, I had a darned sight rather trust my chance of salvation and the country's to the Lord of Hosts than to George Creel—and I like George first-rate at that, and think he's a good fellow. But I have had good opportunities in my time to observe the scale that creation is built on. I have studied the law of moral action and reaction, whereby hatred begets hatred, and ceaseth not but by love. I had much rather trust myself to the operation of that law than to some little ponderous unhumorous lucubration of a few poor pitiful wretches in Washington, beset and bedevilled as they are by all the demons of need, greed and vain-glory. So I positively decline to be frightened or angry and only wish you might see as clearly as I

do, how little there is to be afraid of or angry at. Plenty
to be sorry for,—no doubt of that,—and the most I am
sorry for is when good men like you get bowled out of
their self-possession, for that is what does the mischief.

Think it over, and see if you can't reach other se-
quences for your mind to run in except censorships and
suppressions and force-majeure; they have been worked
to death and have brought forth nothing; nor will they
bring forth anything now but their own natural fruit.
Making the world safe for democracy by those means
has but one historical parallel, that of Buck Fanshaw,[30]
who was a man of peace and would have peace if some
one had to be carried out on a shutter.

Ever of thee,

To Ruth Robinson
BRANCHVILLE, Wednesday,
August 8, 1917

My essay is all right and I imagine I'll have it done
this week. As regards magazine work, I am at present
in a period of considerable discouragement and scarcely
know what is the best use to make of myself. I shall
know better by the first of the week, when I hope to
come up & see you at your work of suffraging. My health
is fine & never better and I don't have to think any more
of hay fever for another year. Wasn't it splendid, getting through so well. But I am a good deal bothered
about other things,—first, the fact that I have so much
trouble in magazine-work, and second, that I have to
do a piece of building up here, and one has to pay something more than two prices for anything in that line.
However, the magazine matter is the big thing. I feel
the irresistible temptation to throw the whole idea over-
board and never to write another word except fiction.
The book, of course, is all right. But there does not
seem to be a magazine that will stand up for anything
like the plain facts of our social conditions, or that wants
the facts presented. They say they do but really they

---

[30] In Mark Twain's *Roughing It*.

don't. At all events, if I finish that series for the Century, I shall not undertake anything of the sort again. It is too troublesome & disappointing, and there is too large a range of life outside that one can deal with.

NEW YORK, Monday night, August 13, 1917

Your two little letters came & brought me all sorts of good cheer. If you think as highly of me as all that, I'm sure I must amount to something after all. But I have been a good bit discouraged & low-spirited these past few days. It isn't that the *Century* won't print my stuff—they are still sticking to it—but it is such up-hill work to get anything past their timidity that I often think it isn't worth while to try.

I am horribly disappointed, but I can't get away until Wednesday, due to that same infernal magazine. Doty[31] came back from his vacation today and I must spend most of tomorrow with him over my own paper and the other matters that I attended to for them in Washington. If I possibly can I shall take the 10:03, but if I came at 1:03, I could still reach the meeting. I shall telegraph you which I can do.

Such glorious weather as we are having & it is hanging on so long—I am thankful & feel I never ought to be unhappy again—particularly the way public affairs are going. If I could afford it, I would drop every thought of magazine work and write for the radical press. The *Public* has increased tremendously and the *Call* has trebled its circulation since we went into the war. Publications like those now have a big future before them.

BRANCHVILLE, Saturday,
September 29, 1917

Warm & unsettled weather—maybe we shall get some more rain out of it yet. That was a curious sort of let-

---

[31] Douglas Z. Doty, editor of *Century Magazine* among other positions held. His wife was Josephine Whiting Doty.

ter I sent you yesterday,—I hope you can make something out of the schedule I finally was able to dig out of the railway guide. I think you may depend on it as correct.

I have been thinking a little about my Democratic Ideals of Peace, and there really does not seem much to say. With economic opportunity set free, men will naturally keep peaceful without anything being done about it. Perhaps the thing to do is to say that as simply as possible, and devote oneself to making it clear. But a glance at Amos's chart is enough to show what hopeless things treaties & international agreements are on the present basis. I think before we are through, a great many people will have learned more about this than they are at present aware of.

Earlier in the week I was reading over again Justin McCarthy's History of Our Own Times, which covers practically the reign of Queen Victoria. I was in search of something to take my mind off my jaw, and I found it in a very interesting comparison of the non-partisanship of the Manchester School with that of our Non-partisan League. Cobden & Bright were good non-partisans, and the whole movement had a purely economic character; and they made the parties come to time. If the right leadership could be gotten for our farmers' league—if they had a few historical students and a man or two like Cobden who could deal with the *theory* of things, they would go an everlasting long way. Henry George could do it if he were alive now—it is unfortunate that he lived at such an untimely time. I was interested too in seeing how much the same sort of man they had to deal with in Sir Robert Peel as we have in Wilson. Peel was abler, more honest and less provincial,—having been in contact with great affairs all his life. But temperamentally they were much alike.

Of course, the great trouble, the notable weakness of our civilization is that from first to last, no one cares for the theory of anything; so perhaps no Cobden could count for much. It may not always be so, but it always has been. It is what mostly stands in the way of our being a great people. We are opportunists—in politics, in commerce, in education and in morals. Three-dollar wheat is all right as far as it goes, but surely the thing to keep one's mind on is free trade and the confiscation of land values. Sometimes I think I should like to move to any country where there was a sense of logic & lucidity, and some kind of relief from the everlasting hypocrisy with which we cover our failure in both & our lack of interest in both. Our failure in logic & lucidity is our most damaging inheritance from the Anglo-Saxon stock, and our miserable canting hypocrisy about it is the most contemptible. I even think I could go to Prussia & be hammered around by the police awhile, if only they didn't pretend they were doing it for the glory of God or to make the world safe for democracy or some other loathsome humbug.

Whoopee!!—so with these few remarks, I'll play me a tune on the phonograph. After all, we have a lot that is sincere & true to listen to, like Bach's Concerto, so why not do it & stop stewing over what isn't?

To Francis Neilson

September 6, 1919

DEAR F. N.:

We have to have your O.K. on a name pretty shortly in order to get out a circular. I go to Detroit tomorrow for Sunday at Ingram's forum; and will be at Oberlin College Monday night (c/o Professor Charles Wager) and return reaching New York early Wednesday morning. Ben[32] and I then gather together every available suggestion for a name, and forge out a circular.

As between Common Sense & The Freeman, I am somewhat for the former, as The Freeman seems a little special. Ben prefers The Freeman, & I am quite well enough satisfied with it. Common Sense would be (I hope) a thoroughly descriptive title, and I don't see that Frank Hirst's preemption of it on the other side really makes any difference.

---

[32] B. W. Huebsch, publisher of the *Freeman*.

Let us know whether you have any inspirations or ideas. We are going over a lot of foreign titles to see if we could gain a good one by translation.

(Confidentially) we can get the Committee of 48's mailing list, which is a big windfall.

Love to all.

Yours aff'ly,
ALBERT

November 14, 1919

DEAR F. N.:

I received your letter enclosing Villard's, about my return to the *Nation* fold. He had already written me, most handsomely proposing the same thing. I do not see what earthly service I could render the public in that capacity. True, the *Nation* has grown greatly these past months, and is now well over 50,000. But it is not the kind of thing I have any interest in producing, nor is there any prospect of its becoming such. It is incomprehensible to me how any set of men could have gone through this experience with trade-unionism without learning one single thing about the fundamental economics of their situation. It was an opportunity to put the paper in a commanding position and they fumbled it shockingly. It's simply incredible that they should have written what they did without adding a paragraph to show that while the socialization of industry may be ever so proper a thing, it nevertheless gets nowhere as an economic adjustment, because economic rent will devour socialized industry just as it devours capitalist industry. Socializing industry means nothing but increasing the number of your shareholders. It does not change the economic basis of industry a single iota.

Think what a strong leader on this theme would have meant, just at the time that the paper socialized its own industry. The Nation has had opportunity after opportunity of this kind and flunked them all, for no reason but impenetrable stupidity. I can't be interested in that sort of thing, because I can't see that it points the way to any solution of the industrial problem. I like them all, and they are kind and friendly, but there is no more chance now than there ever was for anything but a "liberal" paper, and one can't waste energy on that. If I were you, I should write Villard simply to that effect. Why should you help maintain something that you do not believe in?

The Pathfinder is preempted. Your objection to Common Sense is valid and removes it from consideration. Ben & I have set apart tomorrow afternoon for canvassing every discoverable title, and we will immediately report what we find. You are right about the pamphlets: the sooner the better. I think Ben is beginning now to get his head above water.

The Dial is on the rocks, it seems. Knouth, the treasurer, told Karen yesterday that it was a gone goose. If nothing else were worth bidding in, we might get their lease on the house they occupy; it is well worth having. I believe they have a couple of offers of some kind, but don't know any more about it.

It will be a great pleasure to see you at the end of the month. I hope you are keeping well & fit. I had a pretty good time speaking in Detroit, etc., last week, but I am glad it is over. Love to all.

Yours aff'ct'ly.
A.J.N.

December 15, 1919

DEAR F.N.:

I have been more encouraged and spunked up since coming back from St. Louis than any time these past four years. I really feel that the sane radical is up for his turn at the bat and is in the right mood to make a hit. My pamphlet will shortly be ready, and I'll push the others on as fast as possible. It would be fine to get one on the Constitution out of Knox & I'll be glad to try to land it. Borah has written Ben about publishing a book, & it may result in my going down for a day.

The prospectus seems to be received with favour. The poor old Nation is in a bad way. Miss Watter has resigned, and Mussey said to me today that he thought the game would be up for all of them very soon. Villard seems to be wholly impossible. Mussey told me that on one issue this month, it cost them $600 more to get and print their advertising than they got paid for it. There's business for you. The *New Republic* is dickering with our young man Robinson, & also the Baltimore *Sun*, but I don't think they will get him away from us. Ben talks with Fuller tomorrow. This matter of wages is troublesome. Miss La Follette is keen to come with us and I wish we could have her, but she gets $45 where she is and I don't see how we could decently get out of offering her $50 & she is worth twice that; but I know Ben would go up in the air at the figure, and I am as desirous to keep expenses down as he is. Still, it is a question of getting our pages properly filled, & I don't believe we would find ourselves saving money in the long-run by not employing her; so I think I'll take it up with Ben in the morning & see what he says. We'll attend to the housing question as soon as we get a report on any renting possibilities. For my own part, I think buying that Charles St. property would be as sound an investment as could be found these days.

The *Nation* is printing a lukewarm paragraph on the Committee of 48 (on the strength of the N.Y. newspaper reports) which will make them mad as the devil. Those people will be great advance-agents for the *Freeman*, see if they aren't. I surely think the Nation is on the down-grade, & if we can hit the temper of the times at all, we can do some pretty fair business to start with. Costs are certainly fearful enough to scare me, but maybe we can weather them awhile. Well, we'll see. My love to the family.

Aff'ct'ly,
ALBERT.

To Henry L. Mencken

NEW YORK, March 16, 1921

DEAR HENRY:

Thank you for your notes. I wish you would ever let

me get a glimpse of you when you are here. I do not feel competent to do the paper that Stearns wants done, but I have found a man for him who I think will precisely fill the bill and have written Stearns accordingly.

You are generous to my piece about Harding. If they would only put that Airedale dog in the presidency and train Harding to carry the newspapers to the breakfast table in his mouth, then we would have something which we could really call an Administration, Mr. Potash. I have owned an Airedale dog for five years and I know what I am talking about.

Faithfully yours,
ALBERT.

NEW YORK, November 9, 1921

DEAR HENRY:

I am afraid we can not manage this paper of Mrs. Scheffauer's. I wish we could.

You will notice, I presume, that Brother Hylan got a fairish majority yesterday out of his fellow citizens. It would pay Tammany, I think, to stage one reform administration about every twenty-five years. New York got so fed up on the last one that I am sure for the next sixteen years at least, there will be nothing but Tammany on our local map.

Faithfully,
ALBERT

To Ruth Robinson

NEW YORK, Thursday, August 20, 1925

I was so glad to get your letter this morning. Weather here is also *dreadful*, but the papers say it will be better tomorrow.   Maybe won't. I was going out to Branchville today, but find it better to remain here.

Many jobs come my way, some of them amusing. The new president of Wisconsin University[33] tries hard to

---

[33] Glenn Frank, previously editor of *Century Magazine*.

persuade me to be the head professor of English for him, which I'll not however do. I think that is a dreadful funny notion. The *World* wants me for music critic! I begin to think I must be a jack-of-all-trades. I also maybe not do that.

Harpers, however, interest me. Bill Briggs talked with me an hour and a half the other night, to persuade me it was my Christian duty to do that History of Civilization. They also make me a good offer to go to München, to keep an eye on the German book-market for them, and write for their magazine.

So I don't know exactly what to do. We maybe talk it over when I come up, and see what seems best.

BRUSSELS, May 24, 1926

I have been doing nothing but putter along at my work and live very quietly. That work I am doing interests me so much and seems to turn out so well that I believe I can spin it out into a very good book. After I have done another article or two I shall arrange matters, if I don't do the Rabelais, so that you and I can wander a little during this next year, and I write here and there as we go, with observations on places and people. The best way would be to go from one place to another just as you saw fit, without making any schedule that would be binding. Well, we first find out what happens to Rabelais.

BRUSSELS, December 22, 1926

Being in the swing of work, it goes well and quite rapidly. Three magazine articles are done, and when I write another I shall shut off on those for a while, and use my spare moments in an attempt at a short story. Besides this, I have covered the first twenty chapters of Rabelais in a preliminary way, and the principal result has been to show me what a lengthy job it is going to be. The way the days go by astonishes me. But I am powerful happy and easy in mind, and I feel sure if I can just stick at it, it will go splendidly.

I had an idea the other day that may help. I suggested to Harpers that we bring out two of the three volumes, containing the text and illustrations, this winter, and put off publishing the third volume containing the introduction and notes. In that way we might be able to get the benefit of the Rabelais Society's complete work, which I would so much like to have, if possible. They ought to be through in another year. It would be quite regular to take subscriptions for the set of three volumes, delivering the third when completed. I hope they will do this, and I expect to hear in a few days.

Suzanne is in France, hard at work on another book. I got a letter from her from a place called Croissy, which I never heard of. I would so love to see her, and she would love just as much to see me, but we are both too busy to think of it. I wouldn't break my routine to eat lunch with the King, and she feels just the same way. She is a dear, and so able.

BRUSSELS, February 9, 1927

I tell you, I am interested in the news of that painting. I'll bet you have struck something that is going to keep you delightfully occupied as long as you live. We maybe some day write an account of our travels, and you fast do little black and white sketches to illustrate it. That would be a lot of fun. We'll go perhaps back to Luxembourg and over to Lichtenstein, and do nice things. I wish I had put off the idea of working up all these notes into a book until you had come along with the sketches. But I hope we'll have lots of time yet.

As far as I can see, I have picked up just wonderfully in the past six weeks. There is no reason why I shouldn't, with the best food and care and the pleasantest surroundings in the world. I sleep quiet and sound, and I seem able to work to any extent I find necessary. I tell you, it feels good, for it is a long time since I have felt anything like that.

The February Harpers has not come here yet. Queer I should have heard all the way from California about it before it arrived here; but that is the way with Harpers. I have another two articles in mind to send them, and I do it as soon as I get them written. Those cats will come now shortly along, I think. One of my new articles will be literary, on the Art of Making Low People Interesting. I have read two or three novels lately, all about low people, but they weren't interesting. Then I got hold of Pickwick again, which is full of low people —drefful sculch they are, practically all— and so interesting that you would go miles to see them. So I began to have many thoughts about why that is, and I may soon write them down.

It has been very decent weather for January; we have had quite a bit of sunshine, such as it is. But I don't think Brussels is a very good place to stay in much of the winter. I may hunt up some other place for headquarters. But everything else is so delightful that I hardly think I could ever enjoy another place quite so much. I'll be perhaps in that South County some in winters. That will be better. Here we have a little surface freeze once in a great while, that thaws all away by ten o'clock in the morning; the earth never freezes at all. If these folks had been on Kingston Hill a year ago, they would have known something about real winter weather.

BRUSSELS, February 22, 1927

Everything goes splendidly, but up to today, we have had awful weather. Sunday there was no such thing as keeping warm, but yet it wasn't down to the freezing-point. You know the kind. If I were all by myself and had nothing to think about but just what I wanted, I would like to get a tiny little new apartment somewhere and fit it up, and then go over home for a farewell visit, and make arrangements with publishers to send me books regularly. But the climate in Brussels is pretty bad most all the year, and I don't believe I would do well at it as a steady thing. We'll see how it looks over in Germany somewhere. Judging by Cologne, I don't believe the Rhinelands have a very good winter climate either.

BRUSSELS, May 3, 1927

I think I wrote you about suddenly remembering that the 30th is Decoration Day, and that there are Saturday and Sunday coming along. So it seems the smartest thing I can do to go straight out from Hoboken to Branchville, without trying to do anything in New York. There I can get straightened out and settled and get some of my HMT's visited, all in those first few days. Then I'll come immediately up to that South County.

My old college,[34] that has snubbed me industriously for so many years, has asked me to give the Commencement address on 15 June, and also offered me an honorary degree (Litt. D.). So I think I'll perhaps do that.

The weather here is lovely. Nothing like this spring was ever seen in Belgium, I reckon. I hate to pull up stakes and leave it, 'cause I suppose on the other side the summer may be dreadful, as you say they are predicting.

To Lincoln Colcord

[PARIS] September 30, 1927

MY DEAR LINCOLN:

I am delighted beyond measure to hear from you. You were very good to send the book. I had already read it with interest and pleasure this summer, but that only adds to my satisfaction in having it from you; and besides, I am enabled to pass the lamp from hand to hand by giving my extra copy to Brand Whitlock, which I did, day before yesterday. My best thanks also for your recommendation of two other books which I shall look

---

[34] St. Stephens, which later became Bard College of Columbia University, then Bard College.

into at once. May I in turn urge you to read Beard's last book, The Rise of American Civilization, and Hibben's Life of Henry Ward Beecher? You will draw 600% dividends on those two pictures of our society.

It is such good news that you are settled and measurably happy after your afflictions. I am glad of it. You judged right in thinking I am happy too. If you could live among the Belgians for a couple of years, your faith in the human race would be considerably copper-rivetted. When I get my book done, I shall send it to you, and perhaps you will be able to make a lot of uplifting inferences from it. In a word, what binds me to them is their fierce jealousy, resentment and hatred of all authority, first and foremost. By George, they are the simon-pure natural anarchists of all creation, and their rulers regard them with godly fear, believe me! Next, I am all for them on account of their love of beauty and their infernal unbreakable tenacity of their traditions in art and music. Then I like their social character, their immense physical strength and grace, and their physical beauty. The only thing against them is their climate, which is simply devilish. I would give a great deal if you could spend even one year in Brussels.

I had to come down to Paris this morning for three days, which in the words of Rabelais, is a terrible thing to think upon. There is nothing here that attracts me, nor yet any more in Germany. I don't think I could stick it to live in Munich, even. I see no prospect that the newer elements in German society will be worthy of the old; in fact, I look for just the same regression that I saw in the second and third generation of the immigrant '48ers in Illinois. As for England, it seems at last *kaput—ausgespielt*. I always loathed it, and now I can't endure the idea of going there even for a day. But Belgium seems unchanged after the war; I can see no difference, any more than in Holland. I am sure that the Scandinavian countries must be a good deal the same as ever—I hear they are—but I am withheld from going up there, because I can not speak one blessed word of any of their languages—not one—and I somehow feel they would be too hard for an old man to pick up. In

Belgium I manage to worry along on French and Flemish, and of course I know German enough to protect myself when on the eastern border around Limburg. Not in Luxembourg, however, and it was a blow to my pride, for while I don't pretend to speak German so you would write home about it, I did think I could understand about any kind of German there is. But over there in the Grand Duchy they speak a dialect that I don't believe the Lord Himself can understand. They can understand me perfectly, but I can't get a word of what they say.

To Ruth Robinson

ANNADALE-ON-HUDSON, March 4, 1930

I know you like to read Sedgwick's letters, so here is one for you.[35] It makes me sore that Bell broadcasts this thing in this fashion. There's a lowlife for you! I have blown him up about it.

You must not feel uneasy about this work, for it will not fag me out at all, and will be interesting. Now that Suzanne has all the responsibility for the paper,[36] my share of it is a very easy job, and I enjoy it. So don't be anxious. The only nuisance is my being kept away so long. The book is coming on very well, a little behind the schedule, but Harcourt will give us some extra time, if necessary, and I don't think it will be.

To O. G. Villard

April 23, 1930

MY DEAR FRIEND:

I wish I might come to your dinner on the 30th, but I am tied down to an enormous mass of copy due 1- May,

---

[35] A letter from Ellery Sedgwick referring with great glee to AJN's being on the faculty of Bard College, of which B. I. Bell was Warden. AJN did not take kindly to such teasing.

[36] *The New Freeman*, an attempt to revive the *Freeman* under the editorship of Suzanne LaFollette.

and I could not leave it if the whole German General Staff were coming over. I am in hiding, incommunicado, and sweating great drops of sweat noctesque diesque, kaì night kaì day. You are awfully good to ask me, and I appreciate it. My compliments to the Herr General-oberschriftsteller, and I hope he eats hearty.

May 13, [1930?]

MY LORD DUKE:

I wish you would take a bradawl and get behind your literary editor with it.

Two months ago I sent him 20¢ with a request to tear out a review I wrote for your fall book number last October, and post it to me first-class, because second-class mail normally falls by the wayside at the Players Club. I have never heard a chirp of any kind from Vesey St., and by gum, I want that review. If you want another 20¢, tell him to ship it C.O.D. Ain't it? The review bore the very bad title of "Not So Rabelais," for which your petitioner is not responsible—I should have done worse, as I am exceedingly rotten on titles.

I hope the progress of liberal thought is going strong, but not strong enough to bust a trace, or anything untoward like that. The literary section of it will go faster if I have occasion to come down there, so you had better dig up that review. Take notice, this is *datum Novi Eboraci*, given at New York, under my hand and seal.

Ever of thee,
NOCK.

May 25, 1930

ME LIEGE:

My best thanks to you and your asst. lity editor for the pains disposed in my interest.

.   .   .   .

I trust all is well, and that liberalism is a-sweepin'

over the country like a Simoon of the desert. Let it sweep!

Ever of thee,
NOCK.

To Gilbert Chinard[37]

June 1, 1930

MY DEAR SIR:

Thank you cordially for the gift you speak of; it is held in New York until I return there on Thursday.

Leonard Bacon has a kind of access to the Carnegie people that I have not. He may be able to do something with them, and I know he will try his best.

I shall be glad to come down in the autumn. What you need down there is a professorship of poetry, after the Oxford model—five years tenure of office, six weeks residence and lectures every alternate year. I think I'll get some of my friends to endow the chair, and I'll hold it for the first five years. What do you think of that? I should call it a fine job to hold. I always envied the Oxford Professor of Poetry. Next to that, I should like to be a Fellow of Oriel—nothing whatever to do, and all the rest of your life to do it in.

To Ruth Robinson

St. Stephen's College
ANNADALE, DUTCHESS CO., N.Y.
Friday [November 7, 1930]

What do you think of this?[38] I am rather in favour of it because it would give me a mighty good chance to say a lot that I want to say, and if they will let me do it in February or March, I think I shall agree.

But you will be surprised when I tell you I am giving

---

[37] At that time Professor of French at the Johns Hopkins University, later at Princeton.

[38] An invitation to give the Page-Barbour Lectures at the University of Virginia. These lectures were later printed under the title *The Theory of Education in the United States.*

up those N.Y. lectures. They are just that much more than I can do with any kind of justice to myself or anybody else. I was foolish to take them on, and now I must get out of it the best way I can. It is sort of humiliating to have been such a goose, but that is what I was, and I don't mind saying so. From the point of view of high finance, it won't be any sacrifice, either, for I could get as much money far more easily by writing a couple of articles for Harpers.

I rather think you will agree with me that it isn't sensible to try to do too much and do it; and certainly with all I have cut out for me here and elsewhere those lectures would be too much.

Better address me here now, as I won't be in N.Y. for quite a while.

To Gilbert Chinard

March 20, 1932

MY DEAR AND HONOURED FRIEND:

I am truly grieved to hear that your illness persists. My best hopes and expectations lie in the knowledge that you are in the most skilful hands and will have the best possible care. I trust it will not be long before I hear that you are as good as new, and your spirits as well as your health fully restored. Meanwhile you must rely on the great sustaining doctrine of Pantagruelism, which was given to the world four hundred years ago this summer.

It is true that your president asked me to come down and speak about Rabelais, but I was obliged to decline. I am sailing (first of all, for the Isles d'Hyères) in a few days, and am very busy with many matters that must be settled before I go. I could come in October, but thought it more becoming to decline outright than to suggest a date so remote. Besides, you remember master Janotus's saying, "Halt not before cripples—ne clochez pas devant les boiteulx"—how could I, a layman, presume to speak about Rabelais as a physician before your Faculty of Medicine, or how could I speak about him at all while standing in your shadow?

Do you know, I believe Jehandiez's conjecture about that word *calloïer* is sound. From a man who knew Greek as well as Rabelais, the derivation from καλὸς γέρας or καλὸς ἱερεὺς never satisfied either Miss Wilson[39] or me. We looked up earlier uses of the word, and all we found gave the spelling *caloyer*, which is all right. Then we came across Jehandiez's guess. He speaks of the *Monge des Isles d'Or* of the XIV century—probably legendary, and thinks Rabelais may have adopted his title of calloïer des Isles d'Hyères as a playful parallel. "Ne serait-ce pas une simple plaisanterie, où l'auteur semble se donner un titre monastique, tandis qu'en réalité il se donne simplement un titre plaisant. Origine: le mot espagnol *calle*, avec suffixe indiquant la profession; donc quelque chose comme *inspecteur des chemins* [Angl. *roadmaster*] *des Isles d'Hyères*, alors qu'il n'y avait sans doute aucun chemin dans ces régions au XVIᵉ siècle. [There are very few there now]. Mais à supposer que Rabelais soit venu herbariser dans les îles, il a souffert des mauvais sentiers, &c. &c." Probably, too, in Montpellier the Spanish influence was strong enough to permit this play on words.

This sounds very good to me, for neither Miss Wilson nor I can find that peculiar spelling *calloïer* before Rabelais. How do you like it?

I had resigned my work at college, thinking I had better get out before I was thrown out on account of my views on education, and my freedom in setting them forth. But it seems in spite of all this, the authorities want me back another two months next year, so I shall probably return for October and November; which is strange, for I have talked to them as energetically as master Janotus did to master Jousse Bandouille—"baudet, baudet!" However, the life is quiet and pleasant, and I can stand two months of it very agreeably, for one gets a deal of work done at leisure.

---

[39] Catherine R. Wilson, friend and collaborator in the work on Rabelais.

Speaking of the Isles d'Hyères, why do you suppose your countrymen leave those most heavenly islands utterly wild and untenanted? They are the most charming I ever saw.

To Henry Mencken

NEW YORK, August 10, 1932

DEAR HENRY:

About those books.

Now that my Rabelais is done, I think I am good for one more big job before they set me at shovelling sulphur. What I want to do is to make a first-class authoritative and readable study of German culture. There is nothing of the sort in our language. In fact if you look up the bibliography of English books on Germany, as I have, you will be surprised to find how thin it is, except for politics and polemics. I believe that I am about as well equipped as any one here to get out a substantial work that would probably remain standard for quite a while, if I took my time at it and covered all the ground thoroughly. I am perfectly at home in most parts of Germany, my acquaintance there is large, and as you know, I am rather better up than most people on Germany's cultural history and its literature, and also on the whole course of its cultural relations with other peoples. Moreover, you are aware that the run of my principal interest, which is civilization, would give the right direction to my knowledge and studies.

I broached this idea to Harcourt last spring, and he was very strongly for it; he saw it at once, and we talked plans. I told him I could finance myself half way; I could keep the thing going properly half the time, but no more—it would be a pretty expensive job, if done right, and I would not care to undertake it if I could not do it right. He agreed with this view, and proposed to grub-stake the thing himself, dollar for dollar with me.

I thought this was not necessary, because there is a large fund lately established somewhere down in Pennsylvania, for the precise purpose at which this book would aim. I therefore suggested that he should take the matter up with those people and get them to share the cost of getting the book written, leaving him to take on the cost of manufacturing and publishing.

This seemed fair, as bringing in all three parties who had a common interest in the project. He said he would take it up with this fund but beyond writing a letter or so, he never really did anything about it. I think he was diffident, in the first place, and then times got bad, and he was pulling his sails all in to run under bare poles; so nothing happened. I did not see my way to approach this fund myself, being quite unknown to any one concerned, nor did it seem my place to do it. All that was necessary was to arrange an interview with the leading men of the fund, so that I could appear and make my explanation of the project under circumstances which would show that I was not exactly an adventurer off the street, and would get me some sort of reasonable attention. These funds are usually put in charge of a kind of foundation-hound who does not know much and is mostly occupied in standing off raiders; so I judge that Harcourt, as I say, felt diffident about pressing the matter or carrying it over the permanent official's head; and I, knowing how things stood in the publishing business, felt similarly disinclined to press him and have tacitly let the subject drop.

Aside from Harcourt, the only persons I have talked with are Charles Nagel and Abraham Flexner—merely in a friendly way, as old acquaintances, to see what they thought of the idea.

As a side-product I want to do a literary-travel book on Germany. Such books are also extremely scarce; the only good one I know of was done fifty years ago. My work on Rabelais yielded me a perfectly bully one; when Harcourt read the MS he wrote me, "What a combination of learning, literature and light-heartedness!" He has held it up a year on account of the market, I think properly. This was a new line for me, and great fun, and I am glad to find that I can do it. You must keep an eye out for that book next spring; I got it beautifully illustrated by an old friend who did it con amore.

Here endeth the first lesson. Tell me, first, what you think of the project; and second, if you think well of it, what do you think about the advisability of taking it up with Knopf. I would like to talk the whole plan over with you some time in September, even if nothing comes of it.

Ever of thee,
NOCK.

NEW YORK, February 22, 1933

MY DEAR HENRY:

Let me felicitate you on the vigorous and admirable drubbing you gave our public school system. It has been the subject of great comment in New York, all favourable, even in unlikely quarters. You did a really grand job, and I was proud of my luck in being in the same issue.

I am sailing on Saturday, first, for a quiet spell on the Islands of Hyères, and then I think I shall visit around the Mediterranean region a little before going north. I hope you and Mrs. M. will take this route: Rotterdam, Brussels, Luxembourg; visit the Grand Duchy, seeing Diekirch, Vianden, Clervaux, Esch, Bourscheid; then to Trier; then down the Mosel, stopping at Traben (Hotel Claus-Feist, and ask Frau Feist to let you sample my Privatbrand of echt Schwarzwalder Himbeersgeist[40] with your coffee after dinner); also consider the graven image on the tower of the hotel, beneath the upper window: then to Coblenz and up the Rhine to Mainz, Heidelberg, Heilbronn and where you will.

I have nothing in mind to write about for you, notwithstanding I hate to be out of the *Mercury* as long as I probably shall be. When a year of my journal is done (in June) I shall send it to Knopf. He thinks there may be some chance of a book in it. If anything occurs to you that I might try my hand at, let me know. The Players will always forward a letter.

You can get better Spatenbräu beer in Brussels than

---

[40] AJN's German was not always as accurate as he liked to think!

in Munich, where they make and export it. Also a noble light beer—Dortmunder Hausebier. There is better music in Brussels, too, than I have heard elsewhere in Europe. I think you will find the Grand Hotel the most handy and agreeable. My favorite restaurant is the Écrévisse. Chantraine's, just opposite, is the oldest in town, I believe, and powerful good. The Leyman, on the rue Grétry, is also good. None of the hotel-restaurants are good. The Taverne Royale is very pleasant for lunch; while the Charlemagne, in the rue des Bouchers is cheap, good and pleasant.

I hope you have fine weather in the Grand Duchy, to see it thoroughly and at its best. It is the pearl of Europe. The city of Luxembourg has the grandest poorhouse you ever saw—the Pescatore Foundation—and nobody in it. It is worth seeing. The best hotel in town is the Brasseur.

Good luck and best wishes. Start not too late in June. If you don't wish to go via the Dutch line and Holland, take a ship to Antwerp. My favorite ship, the *Volendam,* sails 3-june—just right—and the Dutch galleries are wonderful. So is the gin-and-bitters; the food is the best in Europe (e.g., at the Bagatelle, on the Coolsingel, Rotterdam). You won't regret two or three days in Holland.

Ever of thee,
NOCK.

VIDAGO, PORTUGAL
June 17 [1933]

DEAR HENRY:

Peace be multiplied unto you. I am glad the new beer is not at all bad. Piel made a good brew in the old days. I liked it best, except for a Busch brew called Michelob, which was scarce and hard to get. I have swallowed so much Portuguese beer that the sight of a horse puts me in a most dreadful fright.

I am up here in the "Portuguese Vichy" for a few days, trying to write a long piece on Henry George for Scribners. They asked for it, God knows why. The lunatic fringe of single-taxers hate me like the devil, and when my piece is published they will burn me in effigy. H. G. was mighty near the world's ablest man of the xix-century, and his economics are sound to the core, but he had no more humour than a zebra, and that gave his movement a wrong direction and sent it to the devil.

Well, that is the curse of crusaders and crusading— that dreadful grandma flavour that they get into their literature. I hope God will have mercy on their souls.

To Bernard Iddings Bell[41]

BRUXELLES, August 25 [1933]

MY DEAR AND GOOD FRIEND:

Trooly, you are a noble feller, and I love you with my whole heart. I am sorry I could not feed you properly in Brussels. It went against my grain, for I really know how to do it, though you mightn't think so. But the opera was the important thing, and a really proper Flemish feed can not be hurried. It is an affair of much time and great deliberation, otherwise the proprietor won't let you in his place again. Still, aside from this unavoidable failure on my part, it was really an occasion. You were so good to come down and give the little old Monnaie a looking-over. I am as proud of that house as if I owned and ran it. When you are located in England and I am here, you must come over in the grand opera season, and we will hear something like Don Quichotte or the Tales of Hoffmann, and then go forth and shoot up the town.

Scribner's say my piece on Henry George will be out in the November issue. It is dull, but you must look at it, please, for the view therein contained. Belgium won't be any too far off for me to seek safety in until the single-taxers get through boiling over, but I am sure I am right about H. G. Old Isaiah's notion of a Messiah was sound all the way through—"he shall not strive nor

---

[41] Long-time friend of AJN; Warden of St. Stephen's College, later Warden of Bard College; resigned from this to devote the rest of his life to the work of the Episcopal Church and to educational matters.

cry, and his voice shall not be heard in the streets."
Pretty good, you know.

Well, aside from that, I have just finished what I think
is a *grand* piece—reflections bred in Portugal—which I
shall try in a hopeless way on Sedgwick. Somebody will
print it, I am sure, and I don't know why I should be
so pessimistic about Ellery, except by habit. I send him
something about every two years with no notion that
he will take it, but he nearly always does. I detest writing for magazines, however; again and again I say I'll
do no more of it, and then temptation comes and bumps
me off the wagon. I like to labour over a book; maybe
I'll soon have a good one done.

.   .   .   .

1933 [January, 1934?]

MY DEAR AND HONOURED BOSS:

I am *greatly* obliged for your L. C. article. It falls in
excellently with the present run of my thought. I think
you are wrong in saying that in Europe, only England
holds out strongly for democracy. France does far better;
so do the Low Countries. The distinction between the
patrie and the *republique* is strong and instinctive. The
doctrine of Statism & corporalism is repulsive. They
have been all through it and have had enough. But this
is a small point. Rocco's doctrine of Stateism is very
old—taken straight from the German idealist philoso-
phers of the xix century. E. g.—

> The State is the general substance, whereof in-
> dividuals are but the accidents.
>> Hegel.
> The State incarnates the divine idea upon earth.
>> Hegel.
> The State is the superior power, ultimate and
> beyond appeal, absolutely independent.
>> Fichte.
> The State alone possesses rights, because it is
> the strongest.
>> Hegel.

This is the pure doctrine of the latter-day Stateism.
E. g.—

> The State embraces everything, and nothing has
> value outside the State. The State creates right.
>
> Mussolini.
>
> It is nonsense to make any pretense of recon-
> ciling the State and liberty.
>
> Lenin.

And there you are.

.   .   .   .

I am interested in Berdyaev, but not satisfied. Like
Ortega y Gasset, his disregard of fundamental questions
disables his work. The basis of discussion is not there,
and I think informed moralists ought to introduce it.

My notion is that it is not so important at the moment to try to make people take up with this, that or
the other view, as it is to establish the questions that
must be considered before *any* competent view can be
formulated. These questions are sunk now in an immense depth of ignorance, and until they are brought
up and at least clearly presented, I don't believe the
moralist has any chance at all.

This line of thought was behind my suggestion about
your writing. You are in a position now, for a couple
of years or so, to organize the presentation of a fine
lot of fundamental social philosophy, much after the
Socratic method; and you are peculiarly well able to do
it effectively. You know best what your own line of
trade is, and I don't press this one—I only suggest it
as something you may not have thought of.

Ever of Thee,
A. WARD[42]

---

[42] AJN was an admirer of Artemus Ward and prepared an edition
of his works, *Selected Works of Artemus Ward*, which was published in 1924. He was fond of signing his letters thus or with
"A. W."

To F. J. Nock

[November, 1934]

DEAR F. J. N.:

·   ·   ·   ·   ·   ·   ·

I went down to Haverford to talk on Rabelais—only for overnight, and got back powerful weary. I was warned that I wouldn't have any audience, but the place was bung-full, and as good an audience as anyone could ask for—alert, catching everything, and very demonstrative. I was much surprised—especially since the room was bare, dull, overheated, underventilated, and smelling horribly of old Quakers. This is between you and I. But my experience there atop of what I had at Bryn Mawr made me think that region maybe ain't got so much deadly dulness which people think they got it.

·   ·   ·   ·   ·   ·   ·

Trooly yours,
A. W.

DEAR OLD HOSS-FLY:

Delighted with your letter. I got a fine long one from Peets at the same time. Both of them full of good common sense. It is a pleasure to read such letters, for most of the people who write to me ain't got no common sense, *Oser a Stück.* . . . Your idea is the correct one, concerning the dissemination of culture, and your criticism is also exactly correct. The pleas made for French in behalf of culture are hooey—I know it, for I have seen some of the fellers what make them pleas, and I seen enough already.

·   ·   ·   ·   ·   ·   ·

Trooly yours,
POP.

To Bernard Iddings Bell

December 14, [1934]

MY DEAR LORD DUKE:

Joy go with you to Haiti and return! Don't spend too

much energy on converting the natives, but devote yourself mostly to the *dolce far niente*. Let the heathen rage. I was glad to have your letter, and to read your contribution to the Ch. Monthly. I imagine it is a good thing to call the righteous to repentence once in a while occasionally, but I wish we could also train your guns on other game. I had a curious experience at Bryn Mawr. They gave me as good an audience as I ever had. It is the only institution I have seen in thirty years that moved me to sorrow for the students; at least, those in the politics—history—economic line. They are so darned much more intelligent than their instructors. If I could have those gals for six months, there would be something doing. I spoke to a general audience, and afterwards the special crowd put me on the carpet for another hour or so. My lecturing went well, apparently; at the final wind-up I got five curtain-calls. I gave them the Word with the bark on it, and it seemed to be appreciated—my subject, by the way, being our public affairs, considered historically, with reference to the principle of causation.

I was up in Boston last night with Sedgwick. He wrote me awhile ago for some more papers, but I had nothing in mind at the moment; so in the evening we talked over various subjects, aiding our lucubrations with applejack. We hit on one or two ideas that seemed likely, and I'll work them out, if, when and as I can.

Good luck, my dear friend—a happy journey and a good rest. . . .

Again I say, if the people imagine a vain thing, don't strive too hard to find out why. Let them went. You take care of yourself, drink a great deal of rum-and-cola, and smoke all the native cigarettes that you can get your hands on, eat plenty of salt fish and akee, for thus only shall the word of Truth prevail. Experto crede.

[1935?]

MY DEAR LIEGE LORD:

I am just back in town, and find that you called me— sorry. You were so good to send me the *Ch. Times* with the report of your searching discourse. You spoke nobly, as you always do. How much, how very much, you have done A. D. M. G., and it will be remembered for you in the Day when He makes up His jewels. Meanwhile, don't be above accepting the affectionate admiration of a feller who ain't never done scarcely nothin'.

· · · · · · ·

September, 1935

MY DEAR AND GOOD FRIEND:

Your discourse at Bristol was a great one. The point you touched on towards the end is worth developing— that the more one contemplates God, the less one frets about the *outcome* of human endeavour, while at the same time one's sense of the value and respectability of that endeavour increases. Put flatly in this way, it sounds like a paradox, and the resolution of that apparent paradox into orderly good sense and reason is interesting. You might take a shot at it some day, showing how the vision of God reconciles an attitude of great seriousness towards the endeavour with one of great equanimity towards whatever comes of it or does not come. But you are so right. Our schemes for "improving the condition of the poor" (can you beat that?), economic planning, and so on, have no soul—that is the trouble with them. Well, as I said before, you will reach the remnant, and that is the real job. Do you know Matthew Arnold's essay, or lecture, on Numbers and the Remnant? I suppose so.

March 9 [1936?]

DEAR SIR:

I don't know about this business. Eating with the proletariats in a low joint like the U. C. might seriously damage my status—almost sure to be found out, you know. A person of my position and connexions has to be very careful. I'm afraid I really must decline—and, come to think of it, I expect to be in the South County about then or thereabouts. This city is very vulgar, you know, and likely to tarnish my nickel-plated culchaw. I am not proud, you understand—I assure you of that —but I feel I must consider the sensibilities of my associates. Ain't it?

I wonder how his Grace of New York likes the spiritual company he keeps in Scribner's—me'n Jim Wadsworth. What an extraordinary idea. The boys here at the Club take it to heart, and talk of having me up before the Board of Governors for examination.

. . . .

Feast of St. Barbecue of Limoges
August 31 [1936?]

MY DEAR LORD GOVERNOR:

I'd like it first rate. Truth is, though, I would rather see you than either Cram or Eliot or both, even if you threw in the Prothonotary Apostolic of Athabasca for good measure. I am nearly sure I won't be able to make it, however—certainly not before the last week in September. So I had better say no, leaving it between you and me that if I can get loose we will trust to improvisation, and anyhow—which is the main thing—you and I will foregather in the *old* style.

To S. A. Nock

November 16 [1936]

DEAR PEETS:[43]

Glad to hear from you. The editor of the Freeman is all here. You see, Mr. Palmer says what he likes editorially, and lets me say what I like. That's all I care about. In fact, he wants to have me take up my side of the free speech business, and I shall probably do so.

I like that way of editing, and followed it on the Freeman, printing lots of stuff I took no stock in, but I did so because the fellow (1) had a point, and (2) made it out, and (3) made it out in first-class, high-grade English.

_____

[43] Enright Peets, a character in the *Wolfville* stories by Alfred Henry Lewis. It was AJN's nickname for my brother.

The only other consideration was space, of course, and I often ran a piece in two sections, in order to get it all in.

Meanwhile, good luck. Don't discourage freedom of the press, when you see a fairish example of it. The Atlantic and the Mercury always let me say just what is on my mind; if they didn't, you can bet I would not be writing for them.

[P.S.] Sister Thompson ain't telegraphed me any more.[44]

[1937]

DEAR PEETS:

I was greatly pleased with what you sent me. The piece in the Kansas City Warwhoop (or whatever) is done with an excellent simplicity, straightforwardness, and is therefore forceful. Like Thomas Jefferson, I am "a friend to a judicious neology"; also slang; and in my own writings I do a good deal with both. I don't think either practice needs defense or apology, for as you say, the growth of language takes its own course, regardless. The question of taste might profitably be taken up, perhaps, for it comes in, but that would be a harder job. There is a good deal of smartness in some of our current perversions—perpetrated, you know, out of the mere wish to show off, and therefore disrespectful to the reader. You seem always to be very courteous to yours—instinctively so, I think, and I am glad to see it.

.   .   .   .

Trooly yours,
POP.

---

[44] One day at lunch my father remarked, "If sometimes you begin to think the old man is pretty good, and you feel that maybe you ought to be a bit proud of him, remember this and realize that he ain't so much after all." Then he showed me a telegram from Dorothy Thompson inviting him to meet with Mr. Hoover and others interested in forming a group to work for the restoration of liberal government. This was subsequent to 1933, but I forget the exact date.

To Ruth Robinson

BRUSSELS, BELGIUM,
December 12, 1937

I'm now all settled down to work on that monument and on things for the Atlantic and the Mercury. I won't be going over to Parijs until some time in January, I am sure of that. The fine weather gave way at last, and we have been having a spell of the good old kind; but I am warm and thoroughly comfortable; you must not think for a minute that I am not. I am living *well,* but with things as they are I hardly see how other people manage to live at all. It isn't much like the old days, when Brussels was Brussels, and everything was all wrong, maybe, but everybody seemed a lot more cheerful than now. People tell me that general confidence has petered out, so there is little business, with even the folks who have a bit of money hesitating about buying anything. From the looks of things in the shops I should say this is so. There were crowds around in the week before St. Nicholas's Day, but the actual volume of trade was not large, and now there are no crowds at all. Prices in francs seem rather high, but of course that won't affect me unless Franklin cuts up some more fool tricks with the dollar, which I doubt he will.

I have not been down to see my old Flemishers in the south end of town, nor have I prowled around at night at all, for I have the feeling that there isn't much doing to make it either pleasant or worth while. I was once in the Pourquoi Pas, and once in the Trois Suisses, and found very few in either place; the waiters told me that people were looking at their money pretty closely. Nevertheless it is a good old town, and I am enjoying it— really—though more for what it used to be than for what it is now.

I have the notion, however, that I'm willing to call this my last bust in these parts, and I think I shall come back with the idea of settling down permanent-like, except for what going away you and I can manage to do together as a matter of pleasure, and not trying too hard to combine pleasure with business. Probably

we can do something of the sort now and then, unless
Franklin busts us all up. All the news I get from Parijs
is rayther glum, as you could see from the clipping I
sent you. Holland is doing better. Dutchers told me
they might be doing better still (they always say that)
but were rubbing along easier than their neighbours.
Anyway, I am sure there is small chance of a war, for
I don't believe any of these governments would trust
their population enough to send their armies out of the
country.

I'll write you more of how things are, as time goes
on and I see more. In the course of years, I suppose,
the town will be back on the old basis, but it may be a
long time.

BRUSSELS, BELGIUM
December 26, 1937

Just a word or two in reply to your postcard which
came in on Friday. I am glad to hear that my letters
of the 1st and 6th have reached you, but I can't imagine
what has become of the others which I mailed before
that, from the ship and from Holland and from here.
It is powerful unsatisfactory to write letters, feeling
that you are dropping them out into the wide world.

This morning I was prowling around the south end
a little, just for a walk, and I don't know but what it
is still a pretty good old town, after all, if one can keep
off the north end of the lower boulevards, especially
in the evening. The rest of the city has not changed
any to speak of, and the place near the Potbakkersstraat,
where we got our lunch that day, looks exactly the same.
Our friend Claiborne is still at the Guaranty Trust
(which he says is doing no business at all) and is as
nice as ever. He says a new lot of apartment houses
have gone up lately—far too many—and are a drug on
the market; and I see many of them are advertised for
sale. In fact, overbuilding and overimproving seem to
have been the rule. The new Palais des Beaux-Arts is
a sort of Rockefeller Centre on the Brussels scale, and

is pretty dreadful. I went in there to hear Liszt's Missa Solemnis, and walked out on it. It was shocking bad. The old Conservatory, however, keeps up to the mark under Defauw, though its concerts are very few. I had the luck to get in on one—Pergolese's Serva Padrona— which was very fine; but there won't be another one that I want to hear until the latter part of April, when they do Verdi's Requiem; but I won't be here then. It seems to be an extremely slim season for music. The Monnaie, even, does not advertise anything interesting but Mireille and one more performance of Fidelio. The trouble is that everybody is worried and uncertain, not at all about war, but about the awful difficulty of getting on. I don't want to fill up my letters with this sort of stuff, and I won't refer to it again, but that is just what the trouble is; and until there is some change in that respect, it is not a happy country to be in, which is a pity. Holland is doing a good deal better. I am getting used to it here, though, and I see reason for a great deal of my love for the old place to be coming back, so I shall get on very nicely. At the same time, I shan't look forward ever to come here again for pleasure until things pick up, if they ever do.

I have my job laid out so as to stay here until I get everything done that needs doing in Brussels, and then go over to Parijs for the few odds and ends that can't be done anywhere else. I should be through with them in ten or twelve days. Then I'll hop on some sort of craft and go home. That is the best arrangement, since it seems unlikely that the prolotoorios[45] will break out and wreck the National Library yet awhile. I am fixed so well here that I would rather push on without any interruption and then get out for good; and the longer days (they get longer quickly) would be better for me in Parijs. Here, by some miracle, I have good light, which as you know, one never finds over here. I got out the little old desk lamp that I used to work by in Schaerbeck, and it works perfectly after all these years

---

[45] A term used by Mr. Dooley, Finley Peter Dunne's character, a favorite of AJN's.

of lying idle in an old trunk. I am not finding any trouble about diet, for the good places to eat are as many and as cheap as ever—cheaper than when you were here, because a dollar goes further than then— the franc is as low now exactly as when we were first here, and the French franc is a shade lower still; and I have plenty to go on with, even though a feller couldn't live on only living expenses. Each morning I go into a place near the North Station where they make a feature of good rolls and brioches and breakfast-coffee (mostly hot milk, and good), and carry along an orange. That gives me a good walk before settling down. Then later in the day I nibble something good at the Pourquoi Pas, or somewhere else of the kind—in short, about as we used to do. So you can see how well I get on. As to the weather, I take it as it comes, which is the only way to do, as you know. I agree with the Hollander friend of yours, that if after you get used to it you go out and fight the climate as the natives do, it does pretty well by you.

So far I have had no desire to go out and prowl around evenings, for there is not much doing in the cafés these nights, and nobody very cheerful. Maybe I shall take a look around on New Year's Eve, if it doesn't rain. We have not had a great deal of rain—none of the *old* kind, but a good deal of heavy air and "fodge."

So you see I am doing as well as any one can, and getting over some of the first impressions which were so disappointing. Nevertheless, I am willing to call it square forever on visiting these parts unless under happier conditions.

I'll shortly write again, and I hope this letter will turn up some time. I can't imagine what befell my others.

BRUSSELS, BELGIUM
January 1, 1938

This is New Year's Day, so I write you a little letter to say how much I wish you a happy new year, and very many of them. I am afraid you maybe think I am over in Parijs, fighting off strikers, but I am not. I'm still right here in Brussels and going to stay here for some time yet. There will be enough trouble over there, probably all winter, to keep things in a mess periodically, but it won't be more serious than that. You might tell E. and T., though, that if they are thinking of coming over this way in the spring, they had better give it up. That is the way it looks to me just now, but if I see any prospect of a change for the better, I'll let them know. Things are pretty dismal, and there is no fun to be had, much, for any one who is at all accustomed to things as they used to be. This is true here, and even worse in France, according to all I hear. There is no danger of war, however, or of any serious outbreaks, yet awhile, anyway, and that is something.

There is a queer contrast of conditions in France and Belgium. Here van Zeeland gave too much of the benefit of the devaluation to the industries and banks, and put the prolotoorios off with some fine promises of improvement when the industries got on their feet. They are on their feet now, and the prolotoorios are rapping for a showdown on the promises. In France, on the other hand, Blum gave the prolotoorios too big a slice of the devaluation, and some of it has to be taken away again; so the French prolotoorios are hot about that. Thus in both countries production is held up for exactly opposite reasons—and there you are.

I am all accustomed to things now, and quite happy —anyway, very contented. I even took a look in the Grand Hotel yesterday. It was pretty sorry—you wouldn't want to see it. The head book-keeper and the portier are still there—very glad to see me. The ground floor is all changed—as I told you, the big old lobby is now a motion-picture house—and the new lobby is small and all dudded up like any other hotel—no character at all. The old elevator-man is dead; they said he had been there forty years. I did not see any of the other old employes around; and they told me the rooms upstairs were being made over and renovated.

I also took a walk down around the poorer quarters

in the south end of town today. The lower end of the rue Haute now has a fine new hospital built on it, and there are a lot of "model dwellings" put up there— probably a Socialist enterprise. Well, I certainly don't begreech the prolotoorios all the improvements they want, but just the same I'll take my Bible oath they looked and acted a darned sight happier a dozen years ago when they didn't have any, than they do now. That time, for instance, when I stayed up all night celebrating Pieter Brueghel—you would see nothing like that now.

But I'm now going to quit writing you these sour letters. I'm all right, and comfortable as can be, and very contented. There is no mail out of here for three days, and slow at that, so you won't get this for two weeks, anyway. I hope my letters do finally reach you.

BRUSSELS, BELGIUM,
Tuesday, January 25, 1938

I forgot to tell you in my previous letters that since New Year's Day them lordly cats and the good-looking gals all seem to have thawed out and come to life again. I think maybe the cats were snoozing behind the kitchen stove in December, 'cause it was chilly, but I don't know where the gals were hiding. However they all are out in full force now. I don't think the gals are quite up to the old form, but maybe my eyes aren't so good as they used to be. I notice a lot more flat-heeled shoes being worn now; they look more comfortable, but the gals don't have the same gait that you and I used to wonder at, especially when they were running down-hill over the Belgian-block pavement.

I am going up to Antwerp on Saturday, to hear the Tales of Hoffmann in Flemish. They sing it at the Monnaie next month, and I'll go also there. Gieseking is coming in February to play the piano but that is all I have so far heard of. You bet we were lucky to hear those operettas. I'll bet they were the best ever done. Nothing at all interesting at the Parc so far, or at any of the theatres.

BRUSSELS, BELGIUM
February 16, 1938

Letters now here, all full of radio. I am glad to hear you have put one in on trial, and I hope it will be good. With the improvement in programmes, it will be a tremendously fine thing to have. I don't know anything about the merits of the different machines, so I could not be of much help to you if I were there. I wish you could hook on to some of the programmes I see advertised from various parts of Europe, and I dare say you can.

I had real nigger luck with the Tales of Hoffmann at the Monnaie, which more than paid me for having heard so little good music while here. I was rather blue about it, because a soprano named Clairbert, an old-timer, was advertised to sing all three parts. She is a most capable artist, but her voice is real French soprano, and you know what them voices is, Mawruss, dry like the inside of an ash-barrel. They make you think of the French whistles what they used to toot when the train started. So I didn't expect much. When I went in, however, I saw right away a notice that she was indisposed, and that the three parts would be taken by the gals who sing them regular. I tell you, I was tickled; and the performance was just the very finest you could possibly imagine. Even the conductor waked up and kept it going in great style. I think I shall have a chance to hear Gluck's *Orphée* before I leave here, which ought to be well done.

I'll write Herbert Cherfils before I go to Parijs, which ought to be soon now. When I return to the States I am coming straight down to the South County without stopping in New York at all. Then I can go there whenever I feel like it, stay long enough to do my errands and hop back again; and meanwhile nobody will know I am around, and I won't be bothered. I tell you, I shall be monstrous glad to call my rambling days over.

To Paul Palmer

[May 14, 1938]
Saturday

DEAR MR. PALMER:

That will be fine; any date along there that you and Henry fix will suit me.

Herewith the SOU.[46] The LaFollette editorial will come along in three or four days. Looking at today's Tribune, I am not so sure we were wise in canning that subject of a grievance against Hitler; not at all sure. We can keep track of the news, however, and see if it is worth picking up again. The subject won't die on our hands for quite a while yet, and may grow livelier, even.

How about a new department called Garlands for the Living? My idea would be to get something each month from no matter whom, that knows somebody and admires and loves him (or her) no limit, and will show cause. No effort at criticism or appraisal; more what the French call an *éloge*. Humble people, maybe, or well known, just as it happens. Such personal stuff always interests people, and if it kept to the line it would sweeten up the Mercury and be a good set-off against the rest of the contents, going well along with the nature stuff, which I am counting on heavily as a feature. Such a department, run regularly would take some work— probably too much for you—but nobody is doing just that; neither the New Yorker in its Profiles nor the Atlantic in its Portraits, and I believe it would be well worth doing.

Ever of thee,
A. J. N.

PAUL PALMER, ESQ.

Not to make the subject interesting, but to make him *lovable*—make him seem like somebody you would be dam' glad to know. No harm if the writer slopped over just a little. Remind me to tell you a story of Oswald Villard in this connexion.

---

[46] "State of the Union," a department appearing each month in the *American Mercury* at that time.

[December 28?, 1938]
Wednesday

DEAR MR. PALMER:

I have your note about books. I shall be glad to do all that. The first thing I suggest reading is Matthew Arnold's Culture and Anarchy and Friendship's Garland (both in one volume) more or less on general principles, both to help establish a point of view, and to help construct a method of approach. You also get from it a distinctively English doctrine of Statism, which will interest you especially. Carlyle's presentation is more German than English, Ruskin's is emotionalized, and Mill's, while interesting is Liberal—i.e., muddled. You may or may not be bored with Arnold's book, but if you are, read it all the more carefully and thoughtfully as a penance—Lent is coming on.

I have your notes, and shall labour with them duly. I see that the Lima conference came out exactly as I knew it would, and I have therefore been cussing you hard for the cut you made in my January SOU. The issue is pretty good, all told.

I hope to see you soon.

Thine ever,
NOCK.

NEW YORK
[February 6, 1939]
Monday

PAUL (force of official habit!)
DEAR MR. PALMER:

I forgot to suggest that if you go in for Haydn's quartettes, you might well make a start with volume 4 of the set of records played by the Pro Arte Quartette, which is probably the best in the world.

If you get records of the Kreutzer Sonata, get those played by Thibaud and Cortot, if possible. The next best bet is Hubermann and Friedmann—don't let anybody suck you in on those played by the Menuhins; they are sentimentalized frightfully. When you make up to a lovely high-life Belgian gal, play her the second movement of the Kreutzer, and she's yours without a struggle or a murmur. Old Tolstoy must have been onto that—he didn't overlook many bets in his earlier days. You might pick up his story by that name some time for the fun of it—it is worth reading.

The Monnaie won't give you Metropolitan-style opera. It's the kind of thing exactly that Hammerstein used to do in New York, and Campanini in Chicago; so if you don't care for that sort, don't go near it. No stars, you know; they never worked on the star system. I wish I could be there to introduce you to your first look-in—some things would interest you more than others, as a starter. Perhaps I shall be.

Yours ever,
ALBERT

[February, 1939]
NEW YORK
Sunday

DEAR PAUL:

Better cut out *The Jew,* and substitute *A Lear of the Steppes,* mostly for the sake of the story called *Acia.* But get *A Desperate Character* and *Torrents of Spring* (mostly for *First Love*) whatever happens. I was wrong about *The Jew*—don't bother about it.

You can order these direct from Heinemann—and don't ever be tempted to read Tourgueniev in a French translation.

As for Emerson, why not blow yourself to all his essays, lectures and addresses? He is worth it.

In Plato, I'd suggest starting with the *Symposium,* then the *Laws,* then the *Crito, Phaedo* and the *Apology* —then study around in the *Meno, Phaedrus,* &c. leaving the *Republic* to the last. The thing is to get first of all a clear picture of Socrates himself, you see. I would suggest by all means getting Xenophon's *Symposium* and his *Memorabilia,* and studying them pretty thoughtfully before you start in on *Plato.* And don't bother with commentators, for a while, not even Jowett —get your own impressions first.

Aristotle, in this order: *Ethics, Politics, Poetics.*

Fare-thee-well, old chap, and joy go with you. I won't drop the *Mercury,* as you know, until it is clearly proven n. g.

Ever of thee,
ALBERT

CANAAN
June 4, [1939]

DEAR PAUL PALMER:

There is nothing new to report since you went away; at least, nothing new which is not objectionable, and that isn't new. I have been buried in the country, save for two days (not consecutive) in New York, and four days at Narragansett, while I was getting my eyes re-set. . . . The Mercury is still coming out, I suppose; I haven't read the last issues. The April issue I thought was very poor. I resigned my job on the ground of going away, but Spivak wrote me a letter expressing such personal concern that I felt it would be the decent thing if I weren't too precipitate about it, so I have been hanging on—but I'm sure not for long. I haven't seen Lyons again since that first interview, and I have no idea how he is doing. I'm sure you can't make anything of a Comrade but a Comrade, however, so that's that. I am saying this in the July Atlantic as an *obiter dictum,* but maybe it will be noticed.

The weather is dreadful—we have had a ghastly spring, or rather no spring. Today is cold, with rain and fog. I'll take the Dutch and Belgian climate any time, over the savage climate of this seaboard. That's just what it is—savage—there is a distinct bloodthirstiness in the attacks on one, spring, summer and winter. Tomorrow I go to New York to make a speech; thence to Cleveland for the same purpose—and there, it seems, I am to be given an appalling two-days razoo; lunches dinners, all in the way of forgathering with the local princes of privilege, their wives and concubines (probably), which is a terrible thing to think upon. Thence what is left of me is shipped to Montreal for a reconstruction-period in the University Club before I depart for the coast by way of Ottawa, Winnepeg, &c. God help us all! I imagine I shall have a fine time on the coast, however, cruising about the various islands and entertaining myself with the spectacle of the retired colonels in Victoria. So, if I manage to come through the harrowing preliminaries, you may think of me as doing not too badly.

My H. George will be out on 23—august—it is a good little book, quite satisfactory to me. Spencer's essays will be out in the Spring, with a good chance of a follow-up of Social Statics. I have happened on one of the princes of privilege who has been keen on Spencer from his youth up, and I think he is quite likely to get behind the plan of distribution which you and I discussed. When that succeeds or fails, I shall regard myself as having done my stuff, saved the country, &c., &c., and privileged to retire like Cincinnatus. But what a country to save!—the mere sight of it makes one think with Balfour that the appearance of man on earth is only a brief and discreditable incident in the life of a very minor planet. Tourgueniev puts the same thing more poetically in his dialogue between the two great Swiss Alps—and indeed it may be true.

I hope your anxieties are over, and that you are in a way to some sort of settling-down. Don't trouble to reply to this barren gossip, for it says nothing but that I am thinking of you—and that you know I always do, so I am not giving you anything new or instructive. Kiss little Janine for me, right in the middle of her forehead, and give her my love, and my gratitude for her having so long been so good and kind to me.—and believe me always, my dear fellow, affectionately yours,

A. J. N.

1989 Crescent Road,
VICTORIA, B.C.
July 6, [1939]

MY DEAR FRIEND:

Your letter gave me a very pleasant surprise. I think

your action is wise, and that the course of reflection which led to it is sound. We can all do with a spot of self-discipline. You are right about the way you gave up the Mercury, and about the bogus rationalization of your wish to drop it. Nevertheless I think—for a reason which I have never mentioned—that in itself, your giving it up was a good thing; the only out about it was that you didn't hang to it long enough to give it up quite creditably—I believe, as I told you, that another year would have enabled you to go out with flying colours, and I would have been the first to urge you to go. I was sorry you couldn't see it that way, but I don't regret your being out.

For this reason—the Mercury isn't your pigeon, and never was. In rationalizing your decision, I believe, you did not quite understand what you were trying to rationalize. In editing the Mercury you were always at odds because you could not do what you wanted to do, and knew you could do, and at the same time make the thing show a profit. The Mercury had to be a popular magazine, with all which that implies, and editing a magazine of that character is no job for you to keep an hour longer than was needed to show that you could turn the trick. You were working under serious compromise—very serious—and in circumstances where you knew you did not actually need to do it, which made the situation much more difficult to get on with. You could have carried the compromise through—I am sure in another year—if you hadn't cracked under the consciousness of it. But the trouble was that you felt—I think you weren't altogether clear about it—that you were not doing what you were cut out for; and I knew you were not, and I imagine Mrs. Palmer pretty well knew it also, though she never gave me a hint that she did.

You may wonder why I am holding this inquest. I do it because I am afraid you will take on something now that will put the same disability on you, with perhaps the same consequences; and I hope you won't.

You have natural gifts of a very rare order and of exceptional power; but their free and full exercise will not pay normally any heavy cash dividends, any more than Bach's or Beethoven's did. You would do well to make up your mind to that. But in their development and use you can produce something which no amount of money can either produce or buy. You know that as well as I do. Moreover, you know that as long as you hold those gifts unused or half-used, you will be very miserable, as your experience with the Mercury proved.

So much for that. Now what I suggest (if you will permit it) is that you go very slow about what you take up with—take the most of the summer to thinking over the situation. You are rather an impetuous chap, and under the circumstances a little time spent on taking the inventory won't be wasted.

If you think it necessary—or desirable—to make character with your wife's people, no doubt some one would put you in a position carrying wages enough to impress them—Wallace[47] would, I'm sure. Then you could grit your teeth and take the gaff long enough to show that you could get such a job and hold it—but no longer. At your age you could afford the time. But it should be done on a clear understanding—an open covenant openly arrived at—that it was done on those terms and those only.

The tone of your reference to these matters made me uneasy. I don't like your term "intellectual gigolo." A gigolo doesn't produce anything. I can't see anything discreditable in living on your wife's money as long as you are producing what you and I both know you can produce. You wouldn't need any more than your grub and your clothes—no one does, or mighty little more— and if little Janine didn't see it that way, she is not the gal I took her for. You would be as well justified in letting anybody grubstake you for a serious purpose as Henry Ford was, back in the 'nineties—and if you ask me, I'd say a darned sight better.

So do go slow, and treat yourself reasonably as well as seriously. I'll be back East by 1 - october at the latest, and don't let me find you tied up to something

---

[47] DeWitt Wallace of the *Reader's Digest*.

which means only another bust. I have had some thought of taking the Holland-America's west coast line to Rotterdam from Vancouver this fall, but I won't—and if I can do anything to buck up your prospects by staying another winter in Connecticut, I'll do that—my quarters in Brussels will stay rented, and it won't be a killer if I don't see them before February. Anyway, we'll talk things over thoroughly, and for the present remember old Kutusov in *War and Peace*, with his doctrine of *time* and *patience*.

Yours ever,
A. J. N.

To Bernard Iddings Bell

September [?], 1939

Alb. mag. presbutero ill^{sso} doct^{ssoq} Bernardo salutem in Domino.

By my faith and μὴ τὸν κύνα, most learned brother, thou speakest ἀληθῶς, and I find no deefect in thy reasoning. Methinketh when England and France get through spanking Hitler ad maj^m Dei gl^{am}, they will look very seedy. I never thought they would take on the job after Russia gave them the run-around, and I don't now see why they did. However. It was a great joy to hear from you again after so long a time, but I wish the news of yourself were better. It looks to me as if the church would have even less place than heretofore for a man of quality and character. I do admire your grit in hanging to it, but as for your judgment—well, I'm not sure. You know best, of course—couldn't do it, myself—I'd feel I was being edged out, and wouldn't try to stick it. Again, however—

.   .   .   .   .   .

I haven't a bit of news—utterly dead to the world, enjoying it, and glorying in my shame. I have just come down from a voyage up the coast as far as Alaska, and around the Queen Charlotte Islands. Fine scenery, of course—nothing much else but, and after an hour or so I seen enough already. After eight days I would

oser care if I never looked at scenery again as long as
I live. For a feller what ain't got the primitive awe and
reverence for nature's grandiose masterpieces, y'understand, they get a leetle tedious in large doses. Ain't it?
The voyage is something to have done once, I dare say,
and I'm glad I did it, but never again. The only dif-
ferentiations were supplied by occasional logging-camps,
which I already knew all about, and by salmon-canneries,
which smelt something pernicious. I don't recommend
the trip—take it in a movie some time, and you'll get
it all far less uncomfortably.

> January 7, [1940?]
> The Lord's 'oly Sawbeth,
> and
> The Feast of St. Wagstaff of
> Walthamstow

DEAR FRATER MINOR:
Methinketh you are too gentle with this bird. These
brethren need a heavy cowhide on their rear. As Bishop
Wilson said of most English Christians—those being sich
as he best knew—they need awakening more than they
need comfort. I tell the Ch. Times that I feel utterly
degraded when I remember that my father's parents
were English—as, by gum, I do.

To Paul Palmer

> RHODE ISLAND
> Monday [March 18, 1940]

DEAR PAUL PALMER:
  Lawrence Dennis told me yesterday that you are laid
up with typhus. That's a nice kettle of fish. Why didn't
you make it leprosy or Asiatic cholera, if you are going
in for exotic disorders, and really get your money's
worth? I am told that your's is not the malignant kind;
the louse that bit you was not up to the job—which I
am glad to hear. I am going back to Canaan now, and
shall be in New York about the first of the month. If
you are deloused satisfactorily by that time, so that your

continued existence is no longer a threat to the Community, I'll take a carbolic-acid bath and come up to see you. Please give my love to Janine, and my sympathy—tell her I always had misgivings about you as a husband, but never thought it would come to this. Assure her that if running a Lazzaretto is too much for her, she can always come home to her old granduncle. I won't go back on her.

On the whole, though, perhaps you might better get well and take this as a warning to lay off going to dog-shows. Next time you may contract bubonic plague or the great pox, if not both together. Remember that while the lamp holds out to burn, &c. But maybe it is the Reader's Digest. I always said it is a lousy publication. You can satisfy me on that point when I see you.

I sent you the *Meditations* merely as a literary curiosity, not expecting you to like it. You will agree it is that, I think.

Yours ever, in the darkest hours,
ALBERT

Maybe again you picked it up in Washington. *Gott weiss* sick lice are plentiful down there. You might tell the quacks that this is probably their best bet, and to diagnose accordingly.

NEW YORK
March 26, [1940]

DEAR PAUL:

That's good news, but I wonder you are alive. Lice I could stand it, but four doctors are six too many, and New York doctors bump you off if they don't understand your case. Why not go over to Vichy in a month and clean up under Dr. Houlbert?—he is good. Think about it.

I'll be in N. Y. several days early in April, and I'll be seeing you. I've been snowed in for the fourth time in a month, and am getting dam' sick of it. The snow-plough went through this morning.

My love and commiseration to Janine.

Yours ever,
ALBERT

To S. A. Nock

May 21, [1940]

DEAR PEETS:

. . . .

The war is a queer business—I can't understand much of it—mighty odd strategy. When I went to night-school we were taught that tactics like what the French-English have pulled off are just no tactics at all. Ain't it? They gave the command of the Norwegian enterprise to a major-general who had been out of the service seventeen years, and living in the depths of Poland—probably half full of slivovitz most of the time and hunting wolves. It takes the chromo. The Wall Streeters say that Musso will turn loose over this week-end, but you know what them Wall Streeters is, Mawruss—they likely got it from a soothsayer—Well, so it is.

[1941?]

DEAR PEETS:

When you see Francis, tell him I had a business interview the other evening with a man who said I should positively let him know when I am in town again, so he could arrange for me to have dinner with a feller by the name of Almerindo Portfolio.[48]

Francis called my attention to this name some time ago, but I still don't more than half believe it. The thing is incredible. It cannot be.

[P.S.] Nevertheless I am going to rap for a showdown on that dinner. I wouldn't miss it for a small clay farm.

---

[48] Many years ago I wrote AJN, welcoming him back to New York, and added, "the city of which Almerindo Portfolio is treasurer." As can be seen, AJN was impressed.

January 19, [1941?]

DEAR PEETS:

.   .   .   .

Your idea of an anthology of American humour is sound. I believe that people would take to it. From a publisher's point of view, the trouble would be to find a man of humour who knows *doch* how to edit. Thirty years ago, for instance, Montague Glass's inimitable idiom of the first-generation Ashkenazim was appreciated by people on this seaboard because they heard that idiom all around them. It has disappeared now, and is replaced by the intonation, and arrangement of the sentence, which are peculiar to the East Side public school. So an editor would have to take this into account. The thing could be done, though, and I agree with you it should be, but I'm nearly sure a publisher would make a botch of it through not having a properly clear idea of just what is wanted, and of how to set about getting it.

I had a fine letter from Francis. He still has doubts about Almerindo Portfolio, as I have. Your collateral testimony about the cavaliere H. Purgatorio helps a lot. Almerindo may exist, though such a thing is clearly unnatural and against God. I'll know the bitter truth, however, when I pass this way next month.

To Bernard Iddings Bell

February 11, 1941

MY DEAR LORD DUKE:

I have your kind and delightful letter. What a schedule!—you are as busy as a boy spearing eels. You are right about recovery from a Harvardian miseducation—it can't be done. I am going to drop out of the Atlantic myself, I think. I told Weeks that his style of propaganda is hardest for me to get on with—it has a puking, smirking physiognomy which is most distasteful. I would admire British bravery a lot more if they didn't keep so many writers busy showing us by indirection how dam' brave and nonchalant they are. Ain't it? Weeks[49]

---

[49] Edward Weeks, editor of the *Atlantic Monthly* after Sedgwick.

is running my paper on the Amish soon, wherein I throw some mud at your *conversos*. I am probably a sinful feller to feel that way, but I haven't much use for a return to religion on those terms. Getting back to God because you are puzzled or scared or weak in the knees is poor stuff, to my notion. Maybe better so than not at all, but I'm not sure. We must try to have a look at each other in New York. I seldom go there, but I'll make a point of it. I am wondering whether those 22 million birds who voted for Willkie have humour enough to laugh at themselves. I doubt it. There's a candidate for you! A fellow out West wrote me, "God save America, with such leaders as Roosevelt and Willkie." I replied that I didn't just see where God horned in. The people wanted them, and by thunder, they got them, and if God wants to save such an aggregate of utter worthlessness it is all right by me, but I swear I haven't the cheek to ask him.

Four days of delightful weather—all the grey squirrels in the county are on hand—most amusing little cusses. Also blue-jays and chickadees innumerable around the kitchen door, petitioning for handouts—Nature's own WPA.

To Paul Palmer

CONNECTICUT
April 24, [1941]

DEAR PAUL:

I'm ever so grateful to you. You are right about Marquand's book—the most grown-up thing in our modern fiction. How it takes the shine out of what S. Lewis tried to do and didn't! I read *Apley* and *Wickford Point*, both very good, but this time Marquand hit the mark in style.

Yes, you and I seemed to get the same notion at the same time. It would not astonish me if we found that Franklin has overplayed his hand a little. Not only do Americans hate to back a dud, but they are also great hands to throw mud and bricks at their erstwhile idols. I have a hunch that maybe these rousing defeats for the British may cause a change of heart. You remember how only a year ago the French were the real thing in democracy, civilisation, liberté, egalité, défence d'uriner, and all the rest of it, while now they are just a lot of damned double-crossing, treacherous swine. Such are the workings of the great American spirit when it sees itself having been sucked into taking on a loser. Certainly the country has begun to inquire what the 'ell, since so much of our produce has gone down to decorate D. Jones's locker—29 latest model aeroplanes and the ship that carried them, all at one pop, doesn't look so good, and that's only one. I really believe those enthusiasts won't have to keep up their lick much longer to convince our people that A. Lincoln's view of homeopathy pretty well fits the case. It may yet be discovered by our revered friends and acquaintances that you and I had considerably better ideas about this imbroglio than they give us credit for.

To. S. A. Nock

January 7, 1942

DEAR PEETS:

Your observations are sound and walable, but it seems I didn't make it clear to you that I have not been writing for publication, but only, one might say, as a stunt, to see whether I could do a certain thing which I sincerely doubted being able to do. I don't know that the book will ever be published, and don't care—I certainly shall not offer it for publication. The man who beguiled me into writing it is very confident of getting it published, but I doubt he could, and even at that I may not let it go.

You see, the people who accomplish things and are "running things," as you say, don't interest me none whatever, and I don't care what becomes of them. Also, fighting what Hitler, F. D. R., Churchill, etc., represent seems to me a very dull business, because you have to become just like them in order to eliminate it, and that doesn't suit me none whatever.

To Bernard Iddings Bell

June 25, [1942?]

MY DEAR LORD DUKE:

Yes, Culbertson[50] expounded his scheme to me for four hours on a stretch. When he got through I told him it was perfect—not a flaw in it—and if he could only think up some way to suspend the operation of Epstean's[51] law, that *man tends always to satisfy his needs and desires with the least possible exertion,* it would work like a breeze and give us a new world. If he couldn't, it wasn't worth the paper it was written on—for practical purposes, that is.

For forty years now, I have been putting the one question to reformers, planners, single-taxers, (one of which I am) socialists, etc., etc., and never got an answer: "Suppose you got your system all set up, what kind of people can you get to administer it except the kind you've got?" There aint any. That being so, right away you have three unbeatable natural laws eating away your system—Epstean's law, Gresham's law, and the law of diminishing returns—and your scheme goes bust. My wholesome respect for those laws is what has kept me out of every "movement" to improve society by political action. I believe Henry George's fiscal proposals are sound, just as I believe the Golden Rule is sound—but if progressive evolution can bring mankind up to the level where either is practicably workable, it has a 50,000-year job ahead of it at dam' hard labour. Culbertson *has* done a remarkable job, but that is all one can say for it; practically, it doesn't amount to a hill of beans. I don't know of anything I can say to him directly that I haven't said, so I'll send the précis back to you. My only criticism is the one set forth above. He is like the hopeful bird who composed an elegant fantasia for the cornet, but didn't put in any rests for the cornetist to take breath—i.e., he didn't allow for the operation of natural law.

---

[50] Eli Culbertson, the famous bridge expert, who also worked out a scheme for saving the economic situation; author of "The World Federation Plan" and "Total Peace."

[51] So named by AJN to do honor to a friend of his.

[October, 1942?]

ORNATISSIME FRATER:

Your letter with enclosures is here. . . .

The letter rolled frightfully while I was reading Frances's[52] letter, and I felt bilious. Maybe there is no authoritative answer from the Church to these here now modern problems, but there is a dam' authoritative answer from the Church's supposititious Head, and if any one asks you, I can show it. Ain't no modern problems —they are all as old as the hills. Tawney's game seems to be for adapting the Church to modern society, instead of the other way around. I don't get that stuff—never did—we've been all through it for half a century. Society, modern or ancient, is only a lot of folks, and the Church has no rightful message to Society—if it has I don't know it. We are overdoing "Society" a lot. The only practicable reform I know of is reform of yourself, and that's where the Church comes in. As for teaching economics and sociology in the seminaries, I think nothing of it. Let's have all the economics there is from the economists—and let's have religion from the Church, eh, what? I think so, and from the line of talk you fork out in public, I judge you do.

I hope I can see you again soon. My book can spare me, and there are no beautchus ladies around. The gals in this end of Connecticut are homelier 'ner Sary Ann, and I don't know any of them—and there is no seductive licker about, neither—and the food isn't overly interesting—you don't gorge yourself none. You can rely on a fellow who has lived in Belgium to be a moral man on all counts in this country—one leads a sober, righteous and uninteresting life, like what the Prayerbook says.

To Paul Palmer

June 10, [1943]

DEAR PAUL:

The record is safely here, and I am no end gratified

---

[52] Perhaps a letter from Frances Perkins, who was a friend of both B. I. Bell and AJN.

for it. Also for your note on the Chilean wine. You shouldn't cast asparagus on the Pittsburgh orchestra— I know something about that. Back in the 90's the iron and coal boys heard somewhere that an orchestra was great stuff to make character for a real live town, so they got together with Andy Mellon, and gave it out cold that Pittsburgh, by God, was going to have the best orchestra that money could buy, and make Philadelphia's aggregation sound like fish-pedlars. Yes, sir, by God, now you just stand back and listen, and you'll hear something that you could really call an orchestra.

Well, bless my eyes if they didn't do it. Somehow they got Emil Paur away from the Philharmonic and the Metropolitan (he conducted Wagner there, following Seidl), gave him all the money that was in the safe, and told him to spread himself—and he surely did. Paur was a really great conductor—Austrian, born in Czerno-witz—may have been an Ebrew Jew—looked that way —I don't know. He was one of the old kind, like Wein-gartner, Mottl, Mancinelli—Stock was the last of them, and as great as any. Paur had the Boston orchestra after Nikisch, then went off to N. Y. and from there to Pittsburgh where he stayed six years—then to Berlin where he preceded Muck. When he left, Pittsburgh took on Victor Herbert, and I don't know what happened there. But believe me, in Paur's time that orchestra was really something. It was a great sight to see the steel and coke brigade file in with grim determination to sit it out or bust, for the glory of Pittsburgh's culchaw. But those birds did something, I reckon, after all—and if Fritz Reiner has the thing now some of the tradition probably holds.

I hope you have a fine time up in Maine. The weather here is devilish. I had a run of lumbago from the worst of it, but after two weeks it tapered off.

Once more my best thanks—mighty kind of you, indeed. I suppose the brats will be home soon. Give my love to Janine.

Yours ever,
ALBERT

Your friend John Lewis seems to be injecting a little sense of reality into the mess of mush behind Franklin's eyeglasses. More power to him!

To Bernard Iddings Bell

June 10, 1943

Mei, Domine, I beseech you in nomine Patris, Filii et Sp^tus Sancti, Amen, to lay aside all other considerations and give yourself over to the study of The New Order in the Church, by Wm. Adams Brown. There is something which you could really call a pronouncement— sound religion, no end of common sense and wisdom, and powerful ability. I don't know the gent, but whoever he is, he must be a real horse-doctor in his chosen line, and no mistake.

I take note of your address during July & August —also of your observation on J. Lewis. I don't know the rights and wrongs of this imbroglio, but I am all for John in his determination to punch Franklin's eye. I hear also that the gin'ral restiveness of the proletariats is going to boil over at this 20% cut on the paycheck—and I'm all for that too.

Yours till deth,
ALB. MAGNUS

The Rev. B. I. B., no less

To Paul Palmer

MONTPELIER, VERMONT
July [2]8, [1943]

DEAR PAUL:

You are certainly right about Rose Wilder Lane. It's a curious book. One can punch huge holes through it almost anywhere, but *never* on a fundamental point. Odd, isn't it? On anything basic she always shoots straight to centres, and hits dam' hard. Another odd thing is that while she has the philosophy of individualism down fine, she seems to have got it entirely out of her own head. There is no evidence that she has read the individualist writers, and considerable evidence that she has not—I believe she hasn't. I think all this is a remarkable achievement, and darned creditable. I'm all for Rose. As for old Isabel's[53] engineering idiom, I don't know that I object to it. Being new to me, it gives me rayther a jolt, but I can't see but what it is sound enough, and probably effective. I don't mind a woman's handling that idiom, or any other, as long as she gets results—but in general, on points like that I think my tendency is rather more on the libertarian side than yours is. So long as any one has the goods, I don't particularly care whether they are kept under a bodice or a wes'coat. Ain't it? You see, I'm by way of taking the person for what he's got. It wouldn't occur to me to make up to Rose or Isabel, y'understand, nor neither to look to either of them for the incalculably valuable spiritual assistances and stimulations, understand me, which other women might give. As companions also, I believe they would be unpleasant as seventeen devils. But for what they have, I believe I can take them without prejudice and be dam' glad to accept it.

I'm leaving here now, and should be on Canaan Mountain tomorrow. As I wrote you, I may have to go to New York later in this month, and if I do I'll telephone you at your office.

Affectionately,
ALBERT

To Bernard Iddings Bell

MONTPELIER, VT.
August 5, [1943]

MY DEAR LORD DUKE:

. . . . . .

But what I set out to write about is Rose Wilder Lane's *The Discovery of Freedom*. By all means have a careful look at it. When I read her and old Isabel it looks like a case of *dux femina facti*. Certainly no men are showing any such grasp of fundamental individual-

---

[53] Isabel Paterson, at that time of the New York *Herald Tribune*.

ism—getting right down to brass tacks on its basic philosophy. It is interesting to me, and also darned amusing—see what you can make of it.

Furthermore, if the advance copies of my book come along by the end of the month, I'll be looking for you. Bill Briggs writes me to go down and autograph a few to be sent around in behalf of publicity—a disgusting job. Autographing is low, and onendurin' to a gent with any pride about him. But I'll do it, and then I hope I am really through with that nightmare. Serves me right for going on with the thing after I had satisfied myself at the end of chapter VI that I could do it. My interest (and I was interested) died a sudden death of coronary thrombosis (whatever that is) at exactly that point, and why I went on with it I can't imagine. The result as a whole is so dull and perfunctory that I could hardly stay awake to read the proof. I didn't tell Bill so, but if he sells 200 copies, I'll cheerfully agree to eat the rest of the issue. I'll give you one, *pro forma,* but you won't get through it—you can't.

So I may be seeing you later on. I hope you find an abiding-place. When I think of you there in the dog-days, I remember the title of Bill Nye's projected novel, "Tried out by Fire: or, What Shall a Fat Man Render When he Shall be Tried?"

September 28, 1943

MY DEAR LORD DUKE:

I doubt I can go to Providence. I am here in the hands of the dentist and the quacks, and they are assiduous. But I shall be in N. Y. on 12- oct., and may see you then—we'll post that provisionally, for further light. The dentist is getting on, and the alchemists and chiropractors are disposed to think—subject to change without notice—that I shall survive yet awhile—so I am encouraged to hope I may be out on probation by 12 - oct.

Collisions of opinion on my book are violent and frequent, but their chief merit is that they stimulate sales. Your notion of my wearing a mask and being aghast at tragedy seems to me exceedingly odd. Why should I wear a mask?—I can't imagine. Besides, how can one wear a mask without knowing it—as how can one be aghast without knowing it? And what is the tragedy to be aghast at? I don't know of any. Show me the first sign of a break in the order of nature, and I'll be the most aghast fellow you ever saw—even the thought of it makes me creepy-crawly. But what is orderly, regular, inevitable, ain't no tragedy to me, and that one should be aghast at it is something I don't understand at all. Some bird in the Providence Journal associates me somehow with "bitter despair"—which I never felt in my life. All this is very amusing, and I don't mind it in the least—quite the contrary, but it also seems very strange.

As for the ladies, you see, I am up on the literature of the subject, as developed and codified in the twelfth century, in the Provence. It is extremely interesting and valuable, and not very generally known. The modern French view of marriage runs straight back to the Thirty-one Articles of the *Laws of Love*—although I dare say very few Frenchmen are aware of it.

I took up with Cram's[54] theory just as I do with Copernican astronomy, because it accounts for everything otherwise unaccountable. I hold it provisionally, like all theories. Show me another which will do as much and do it better, and I'll drop Cram's instantly. So far, no one has done this. Quite against your conception of Cram's theory, it makes the sub-human—as the raw material of the human—immensely precious—and I said so plainly. It is the only theory, as far as I know, which offers a rational ground for this view of the sub-human. So it seems to me that your animadversions are not well-founded.

I distinctly do not pretend to classify myself as psychically-human. No one can cite a word or line to the contrary. I pretend only to know the human being when I see him—just as I darned well know an oyster

---

[54] Ralph Adams Cram, architect and author, whose article in the *American Mercury* for September, 1932, "Why We Do Not Behave Like Human Beings" shook irrevocably AJN's belief in the inevitable self-betterment of mankind.

when I see one, though I couldn't define an oyster in scientific terms to save my life. My knowledge is based on an aggregate of reading, observation and experience —nothing but that.

What you say of Jesus brings out Mr. Justice Stare-laigh's famous ruling that what the soldier said isn't evidence. In the first place I don't paint him as a cross between Matt Arnold and Thoreau; no one can say in any kind of seriousness that I do. But that is small matter. You say he was *not* the sort of being I paint him. Well, that's your privilege, and you may be quite right. But whether you are right or not is strictly a matter of evidence, and so far as I know of no evidence against the view expressed in my book.

Returning to your observations on Cram's theory, I certainly don't know "that man is superior in terms of his philosophic detachment." I also quite agree that "maybe there is something *more human* than intellectual detachment." But bless me bloomin' eyes if I see where all this comes in.

Golly, no—I don't lay claim to be psychically human. "Just because a feller does business as the Eagle Pants Company, he don't necessarily got to be an eagle."[55] You ecclesiastical chaps are great fellows for going behind the returns, and there is nothing one can do about that. I have a bad enough time to get on with what I am, think and say, without dealing with what somebody thinks I am, what I think and what I say.

.   .   .   .   .   .

My love to Mme B., and tell her to look up my authorities. I ain't so adolescent as she thinks, not by 700 years.

To Paul Palmer

October 4, [1943]

DEAR PAUL:

I wish I might be with you and Henry tonight, but the shamans and C. S. practitioners demonstrated over the idea of loosening up on me, and decided that it was

---

[55] Another quotation from the Potash and Perlmutter stories.

a delusion of mortal mind induced by malicious animal magnetism, and therefore displeasing to our Heavenly Father. No report from on high has come in yet, but they say they are encouraged to hope my ticket-of-leave may be validated by the celestial bureaucracy in about a week; and I hope it will be. I have to be in N. Y. on the 22^d, and I suggested that date to Henry; but it seems that the gin'ral restiveness of the proletariats is making trouble for him in some way—probably printers—and he must stand by.

I get sore when I think of what I am missing; but if the chiropractors suspend their death-dealing activities, things may yet be better.

All my love to Janine.

Affectionately,
ALBERT

I hope I haven't stung you in the matter of The Fool of Venus. Your friend Marquand has come through again.

To Rose Wilder Lane

CANAAN October 23, [1943]

Your view of the nature and function of history is, in my judgment, admirably correct. On that account I venture to expostulate with you most forcibly, in the hope that you will not take the course you propose to take. I believe you are egregiously wrong in permitting your opinions to go without every available evidence of the support which history gives them; that is, of course, good history, sound history. I believe that by following the technique which you propose to follow you will destroy half the force of your work. I earnestly hope your good sense will prevail over such a shocking aberration, and that you will do nothing of the kind. Your immediate effort will not be promoted by your leaving out history; quite the contrary; and if it were, I should say immediacy is questionable, even at that.

For, if I may make the suggestion, it does not appear to me that your immediate effort should be to "get a little practical sense into some American heads." I am sorry you have persuaded yourself that you have any such mission. Your immediate effort and your final effort should be one and the same;—the effort to work out your findings thoroughly and in full, to set them forth competently, and let the subject-matter of them form its own appropriate mode of expression, dismissing every thought of who may read what you write, and of what the effect on a reader may be. Never concern yourself with the American mind or any other sort of mind. Your concern is only with a clear, cogent exposition of truth and fact as you sincerely believe them to be. I imagine that for a person of your temperament it will be extremely difficult for you to school yourself into a state of not caring two straws whether any one reads you or not; but I assure you that if you can bring yourself up into this atmosphere of pure disinterestedness, you will give your work an acceptability and a carrying-power which it can get by no other means.

Please take the first page of your letter to me as a guide in composing your next book. I return it to you for that purpose. Nothing could be better, so follow it implicitly. I hope you will not resent the strong grandma flavour of this excursus, and I believe you will not.

To Fred P. Jeffrey[56]

CANAAN, December 14, [1943]

I have your information of Dr. Crew's report that by natural processes a functioning cock has metagrabolised itself into a functioning hen. Perhaps Livy's skepticism on this point was unwarranted, after all. The changes which I have seen taking place in the American people's collective character have convinced me that almost any apparent miracle may occur in the purview of animal genetics at almost any time.

---

[56] Several of the letters included in AJN's manuscript were obviously to people who had written to him after reading the *Memoirs*, but about whom I can ascertain nothing. This letter is one of them.

To George P. Bissell[57]

CANAAN, December 30, [1943]

I am moved to write you a line of friendly gossip by way of salutation for the new year. You must not take it as demanding a reply, for you have work to do and should not encourage idlers to waste your time. I was glad to have your note of the 21st, with your amusing version of Merriwell Modernised. I hadn't heard that the European conference[58] left Franklin and Winston a bit on the outs, but I suppose it may be remotely possible that Winston's demands might become too much for even the most diligent and obedient of servants. What amused me was Comrade Joe's alacrity in signing up with our sweet and lovely brother Benesh the minute the newspapers' hullabaloo about the conference was over. Comrade Joe is a man of humour, and if his humour sometimes takes a saturnine turn, it is none the less enjoyable for that. For my part, I say just as you say, that he is cordially welcome to the whole of Southern Europe's Great Flea Belt with as much of Asia as he thinks he wants.

I haven't heard whether Winston is over his run of pneumonia, but no doubt he is. I believe Satan has had it in mind to foreclose on him one time and another, but the boys talked it over and told him they weren't sure public opinion would stand for it,—better go a little slow. What a pity Winston's old crony F. E. Smith didn't live to see him at his best! There was truly a *par nobile fratrum* for you—Winston and Galloper Smith! You and I will never see their like in this world again, and we won't meet them in the next for we shall be too far up the alley when they come in sight.

January 30, [1944]

Take a look at the leading article in Harper's.[59] I'll

---

[57] A businessman in Wilmington, Delaware, as far as I have been able to ascertain.

[58] At Cairo, ending 1 December [AJN's footnote].

[59] "A Close Look at Roosevelt," by George W. Martin [AJN's footnote].

bet the writer is a Liberal; no other kind of imbecile could do it. He draws the portrait of an ignorant wastrel, a complete and finished ne'er-do-well, and ends by declaring him a great man, fit to stand besides Marcus Aurelius and Pericles!

Can you beat it? I never use the *mot de Cambronne,* —what E. L. Godkin, in his elegant way, used to call "the excrementitious expletive,"—but I do believe, as an old friend said when he lost a full set of false teeth in Long Island Sound, that it seems to be "the only word a person can articulate properly under the circumstances." One can't dignify a thing of that kind by being annoyed or indignant;—your attitude and mine, the attitude of amused indifference, is the only one a civilised person can take.

I entirely agree with you about Lin Yu-Tang's forecast. How in the world can a rational being expect any other outcome? The republican movement in China appears to me to be strictly a proprietary affair, as much a family concern as the du Pont Company. In its bearing on us it is literally what the French call a *chinoiserie,* with no other end in view than that of lining the family's pocket at our expense, and setting up an apparatus of profitable economic exploitage in the future. I think you will see it turn out that way, though I am judging only by the one method I always apply in such cases. When I want to get the measure of any situation arising in the course of public affairs in any country, I invariably ask myself, "If I were a Chinaman (or an Englishman, Frenchman, or whatever) and a crook, what would I do?"—and I form my judgment accordingly. For thirty years my friends have wondered at the correctness of my conclusions, and indeed I have sometimes wondered at it because my one and only method of arriving at them is so childishly simple; yet in all that period I am sure it has not failed me half-a-dozen times, and precious few political forecasters have done better than that, even those who more or less make a business of it.

But I have no great feeling against our being swindled by our jobholders for the benefit of the Soong family, the British imperialists, or anybody else. I could never see the point of getting up a great sweat of sorrow over the plight of suckers, in any circumstances. Our people have had plenty of warnings and plenty of opportunity to find out what their job holders are like and what they are up to; and if the Soongs are smart enough to pull our legs as successfully as the British do, I don't see why they shouldn't.

To J. Howard Rhoades[60]

January 30, [1944]

I am indeed sorry you are having trouble about getting hold of a copy of my book. You might try another bookseller; try Brentano—he would be as likely as any one to have it. But there have always been great gaps between the several printings, during which it has been impossible to find. I marvel that so many people have had the persistence to keep after it.

I doubt that Harper's are suppressing the book on account of its content, though that they have treated certain books in a despicable fashion I can't deny. I always held it against them that they let Douglas Campbell's great book, *The Puritan in Holland, England and America,* run through four printings, and then suddenly took it off the market. That was some years ago. I presume their English branch made difficulties about it. That book is hard to find now, but if you ever have the chance to pick it up at second-hand, by all means do so; it gives a vast amount of highly valuable information, not to be had elsewhere, and much of it quite contrary to received opinion. In the case of my book, however, if it were to be quashed, I doubt it would have been let run into a second edition. Still, our censors may have taken some time at spelling their way through it. My notion is, though, that a much more powerful enemy than the censorship was against it, i.e. Gresham's law; and there is no doing anything about that. You see, the value of literature, as with currency, is determined by the worst form in circulation. Publishers must live

---

[60] See footnote 56.

—at least, this is a general belief—so with their supply of paper greatly reduced, it obviously pays them better to concentrate on books for which they see a continuing mass-demand. I did not expect my book to be published at all; and when it was, I had no notion that any one would read it, and was astonished that the demand for it was anything like what it turned out to be;—astonished and a little uneasy, for I suspected there must be a screw loose in it somewhere. So if it goes by the board now, I could have no complaint, even if I were more interested in the matter than I am.

I am delighted to know you are a man of music. We might have a good bit to talk about if we ever found ourselves together. You should some time assemble your "fiddlers three," like Old King Cole, and give me a taste of your quality. I have rather a one-track love in quartettes. After listening to whatever others, it is pure delight to hear Haydn turn loose and show definitively how the thing should be done. Of all the great ones Beethoven's give me least pleasure. Sinful fellow, eh? I suppose so, but there it is. The other day I heard the Philharmonic do Roussel's Third:—strange stuff, I don't understand it. It reminded me of Wortman's[61] cartoon of a woman leaning out of a tenement window, and calling across the court, "Hey, Annie, how do you tell when sauerkraut's gone bad?" I believe any ten of the strings could play their notes as sour as swill almost anywhere in that symphony, and if the Lord Himself were conducting He wouldn't know the difference,—couldn't know it. I see our Belgian conductor has taken over the Chicago orchestra; the best choice possible, I think. Coming after Stock and Theodore Thomas, he has a tremendous pair of shoes to fill, the largest in the world, but I believe he will pretty nearly do it, more nearly than any other could do, at any rate.

---

[61] Denys Wortman of the New York *World* and its successors.

To Paul Palmer

January 31, [1944]

I have been thinking in a desultory way about civil liberty lately. I doubt that one in 100,000 of us has anything remotely like the conception of it that you and I have. I believe that for the immense majority of people liberty means only the system and the administrators they are used to. What do you think of that idea?

For instance, the Scots clansmen had their feudal or semifeudal chieftains who certainly pushed them around plenty enough, and made them sweat. The English came and ran out the chiefs, and took over the job of pushing the clansmen around exactly as before; and then the clansmen put up a tremendous roar about losing their liberties, which in your view and mine they never had. Isn't it so? I don't know but what the great libertarian movements might profitably be examined in the light of this notion. I know it must have been dam' disagreeable to the Gauls to have *le vieux César Brisetout* busting in on them, and all that; and as a matter of sentiment I'm in favour of Arminius, Ambiorix, Ariovistus, Vercingetorix, & Co.; but what I should like to know is, how much actual liberty did the Gauls lose? Or again today, if King George or Hirohito or any one else conquered us, ran Franklin and his banditti into the Potomac and put us under the identical régime that we are now under, we would raise a frightful row about the loss of our liberties, when actually we were losing none.

This idea seems to reach pretty far in one direction at least. If people grow up in adjustment to a system and are told that they have their liberties under it, the natural thing would be for them to think they have, for they would have nothing to true the statement up by, and it would not occur to them to test the statement by an exercise of imagination. What will a child think fifty years hence when he is told of a time when he would have been free to shine shoes or sell peanuts without benefit of bureaucracy, or to sail for Europe with no passport and no questions asked? I doubt he will take it as at all reflecting on his own condition, but only as a matter of vague antiquarian interest, like the fashions in bustles and bathing-suits.

If there be anything in this notion, one is bound to wonder what use there is in talking about liberty as a principle. I doubt there is any use; apparently it stands to reason that there isn't.

I have just now had notice to be in New York on Thursday. Could you stick a dinner at the Armenian's that night? Mussels, artichoke, tanaboor, lamb's knuckle, egg-plant, wheat pilaff, Greek cheese. I'll take you wherever you say, of course, but I mention this place because it is the only one I know of that has held up;—at least, the food was good as ever, two weeks ago.

The Balkan Restaurant, 129- East 27th St., just west of Lexington Ave., north side; say 7:15 or thereabouts. I'll telephone you Wednesday evening around 6:45.

Going down is an infernal nuisance. That old project of an issue of pamphlets has come up again; and besides that, I am wanted for a conference on education at the Princeton Club!

God help us all!

Yours ever aff'ately
ALBERT

To Albert Engel[62]

CANAAN, February 29, [1944]

Your letter gave me a great surprise, and a most welcome one. I should have replied more promptly, but I have been away for a week and have let all my correspondence lie untouched. You were very courteous to write me in English, and you were wrong in feeling any uncertainty about it, for your English is exceedingly good. But since we both understand each other's language so well, why should we not each write in his own native tongue and idiom? Matthew Arnold, who wrote very good French, used to write letters in English to M. Michelet, and Michelet replied in French; and I

[62] A French-born businessman who married a friend of AJN.

think in our case that would be the better way. I am
interested in your comment on Proust, and think you
are exactly right. I never have read him without being
reminded of the kind of French that Louis-Napoléon
used to speak; or Franz, in Offenbach's *Vie Parisienne*.
Did you ever hear that once when Louis-Napoléon was
decorating a veteran, a wicked staff-officer put his French
down phonetically in the official report? *Fous êtes técoré
de Chuillet; fous tefez être un prafe, che fous técore.*
Nevertheless I believe that Louis-Napoléon was ten times
the man his uncle was. The trouble was that while as
a European he was a very great man,—the greatest of
his time in the public life of any country, I believe,—
he was not a great Frenchman; and what Europe needed
in his place just then was a great European who was
also a great Frenchman. At that, in one or two ways
he was a great Frenchman; but in other most necessary
ways, he was not.

I read Jaeger's *Paideia* when it first appeared. Jaeger
is a first-class scholar of the great old German type. I
dare say he is the only one left. I have immense respect and admiration for German learning, but I am
glad I was not brought up in their tradition. In the
realm of criticism their scholarship so often shows a
peculiar and unaccountable ineptitude, as for instance
when F. A. Wolf, of Halle, launched his theory of a com-
posite authorship of the Homeric poems, and Lachmann
divided up the Odyssey into eighteen distinct produc-
tions. All that sort of exactitude seems very dubious,
for if there were ever eighteen people capable of producing that order of poetry, it strikes me we should
have heard from some of them; and if the eighteen all
existed at the same time it would be still more remarkable. The unmistakable evidence of single authorship is
the *grand manner*, for nature has been confoundedly
stingy about producing first-class artists capable of working exclusively and continuously in the grand manner.
In all the departments of art put together, sculpture,
music, painting, literature and all, the number of such
artists does not come anywhere near eighteen; and Homer
is one of them. A purely literary criticism would catch

the evidential value of that point at once; and the defect of German scholarship has always seemed to me its unhandiness with literary criticism.

To George P. Bissell

March 19, 1944
Later, at CANAAN

Nothing could be pleasanter than to find a greeting from you on my return from New York. I send back the clipping. The lady is right about finding the formula in *Progress and Poverty,* but I doubt that George was the first to use it; I rather think Spencer was, but I am not sure. Anyway, it has been common property for a long time, usually under the name of the "law of parsimony," which always dissatisfied me as being fanciful and more or less misleading; so for the reasons I gave in my citation of it I rechristened it Epstean's Law.

The course of study I described was pursued in an under-graduate college, not a university; St. Stephen's College, up in Dutchess County, organised on the Oxford model. I proceeded bachelor of arts there, and subsequently master. The college went out of existence presently, as I explained in my *Memoirs.* My graduate studies were done here-and-there, piecemeal, wherever I found a man under whom I wished to work on some special subject—Hebrew, Hellenistic Greek, Latin inscriptions, &c. In the course of it I proceeded doctor in the *belles lettres,* but there was nothing unusual about any of that. My only academic distinction worth speaking of is my bachelor's degree from St. Stephen's College, and my pride in that has mounted with the years. On any academic occasion I have always refused to wear any but my bachelor's gown and hood,—rather a silly bit of cussedness, maybe, but considering the quality of scholarship they represent, by golly, they make all the assembled regalia of the modern Ph.D.s and LL.D.s look like Confederate money.

To Elizabeth Lange[63]

CANAAN, April 3, [1944]

DEAR BETSY-JANE,

As you suspect, the death of my dear old friend Hendrik Willem has left me a little low in my mind, coming as it did so suddenly and on top of an unusual weight of adversities of one kind or another. I am sure it was distress that killed him. You see, he was born in Rotterdam, and his family had held a sort of feudal position for ages at Veere, on the island of Walcheren; so all his attachments were torn up by the roots. He was one of the kindest, most generous, and most lovable of men; I never knew one more acutely sensitive to the distresses of other people. He wrote me several long letters lately which leave no doubt in my mind that the ever-present consciousness of sorrow and suffering shortened his life by a good ten years. His great misfortune was his utter inability to "regard mankind as *being what they are*," and therefore he put expectations on them which they are ludicrously unable to meet. I shall miss him as I miss others who were so distinctly superfluous men in our society, but that is one of the penalties which nature puts upon advancing age, and I accept it as such without complaint.

To Felix M. Oliva[64]

CANAAN, May 16, [1944]

I am greatly obliged to you for your most gracious letter. I never read the books of Chesterton to which you refer; in fact, I have read only a very little of what he has written. As for my own work, most of it has been done by others before me. My only contribution is in showing something of the enormous scope of three great natural laws outside the field of economics. I believe I am the first to have done this, though it would be strange if some one had not anticipated me; but as far as I know I am the first. I think also that I am the

[63] See footnote 56.
[64] See footnote 56.

first to carry out Mr. Cram's theory of man's place in nature to its logical length, and to show how extremely serious, even revolutionary, its inescapable implications are.

This is all for which I can claim any originality. It has interested me to see that in all which has been said about my *Memoirs*, no notice whatever has been taken of these positions, basic as they are. They have not been discussed, apparently not even examined. This seems strange, for I have shown that they are intellectually respectable and merit consideration.

The work you are kind enough to suggest is not for me to undertake. I can't propose a remedy for the ills of society at present displayed, because I know of none. The whole point of my *Memoirs* is to show cause for my firm belief that there is no remedy for these ills which by any conjuration could become practicable; the thing is *ex hypothesi* impossible. I hoped that my book would make this belief and the reasons for it abundantly clear, but it seems not to have done so.

Your letter makes me wish once more that I knew your native language and its literature. If I were twenty years younger I would apply myself to Spanish and settle in one of the Spanish-American countries. But I am too old for anything like that now; too old and too broken in body and in mind.

To Merwin K. Hart[65]

CANAAN, June 5, [1944]

The only thing one can do about this fellow is to tell him he is a Fascist, isolationist, anti-Semite and an s. o. b. from the ground up, because he is right. His conclusion that in trying to re-establish constitutional government you are playing Canute's game of attempting to sweep back the tide, is quite correct in my opinion. I would not know what to say to him. The time for building a seaworthy dyke against collectivism ran out

---

[65] Lawyer, and at the time president of the National Economic Council, Inc.

about 150 years ago. Nevertheless, for the sake of the record, I suppose it is all well enough to go through the motions, but that is all that can be done. I'll not make him any reply.

To Bernard Iddings Bell

CANAAN, June 5, [1944]

As against the dog, I am in favour of the cat, having had largely to do with both in my time. The dog is nature's prize collectivist and authoritarian; he has the slave-mentality and can't be happy out of servitude, a natural-born New Dealer, you know, utterly lovable and devoutly given to all good works, y'understand, but a ding-busted fool like your friend Henry Wallace, understand me, so you are devoted to him and all that, but you haven't a grain of actual respect for him, not a grain; now, have you? You haven't, because he has no respect for himself, no dignity. The cat, on the other hand, has oodles of self-respect and is bungfull of dignity. He is an individualist and has no illusions about the social order. The greatest good of the greatest number does not interest him. He takes no stock in any scheme of enforced coöperation, none whatever. He wastes no sentiment on mankind for he knows that mankind is a most dreadful washout, utterly unworthy of his attention. So one is bound to respect the cat, though one may not like him, and when he turns his calm and experienced gaze on the world around him you can bet he has got its measure.

It is the vestiges of the early Socialism and authoritarianism still at work within your *Unbewusstsein* which sets you against the cat. Have you noticed that his friends are always the great libertarians, Mark Twain, du Pont de Nemours, etc., and that it is the individualist liberty-loving peoples with whom he is ace-high, the Belgians, French, Moors, Chinese? There is reason in all this. *Abyssus abyssum vocat.*

To Nancy Scott[66]

CANAAN, June 30, 1944

Thank you for your letter. There seems not much to say in reply. In stating your views of education, nature, marriage and the people of your own generation, you are entirely within your rights, and I should be the last to dispute them. Also you may be within your rights, since the law of libel would hardly apply, in crediting me with opinions which notoriously I do not hold. For example, I do not dislike man-made society; I have made it perfectly clear that I am very fond of it. I dislike bad society, society so poorly organised as to live consistently and contentedly at an extremely low level; and I have also made that clear. I do not hold that love and marriage are inconsistent; whether so or not is a matter of the individual instance. I merely observe that *for me* there are obvious advantages in keeping the two ideas free from illogical confusion. If you dissent from this you are once more wholly within your rights, and as far as I am concerned you shall have them.

So you see there is really nothing to be said. I did not write to inform, enlighten or impose my opinions on any one; nor would I do so under any circumstances. I merely made record of certain observations and principles which have been contributory to the formation of one person's philosophy of existence; with no desire whatever, as my Preface[67] shows, that any other person would accept them or take any account of them. Nothing more than that.

To E. H. Moore, Senator from Oklahoma

CANAAN, July 3, [1944]

I am greatly obliged to you for the copy of your radio-address of 27 May, which found its way to me from your office. Permit me to say that I think it is most admirable; it is thoroughly sound, just, cogent, and its

---

[66] See footnote 56.
[67] To the author's *Memoirs* [AJN's footnote].

tone and temper command my unqualified respect and esteem for its author.

I must observe, however, that responsibility for our government's present status as a collectivist autocracy rests wholly with the Congress. It would have been perfectly competent at any time these twelve years for the Congress to meet any approach to Executive tyranny with articles of impeachment drawn up and presented within forty-eight hours. In my view, the Ward[68] case is merely one more treasonable and contemptuous challenge, not only to the authority of the Congress, but to its power. I am sure you will not misunderstand me when I say that if I see this challenge met with appropriate action I shall believe that the Congress is in earnest about maintaining its Constitutional character and rights; and if not, then not.

To Estelle Roege[69]

CANAAN, July 24, [1944]

You are wonderfully good to make the offer, but I feel as you do that your sylvan dell would be no place for me, though the spectacle of you doing the heavy mother would be no end diverting, I admit. Your high-pressure devotion to that rôle always impressed me as consid'ble synthetic, for some reason,—maybe because I credit you with more sense than you actually have, and the deficit shows up at this point. To me, inescapable youngsters, especially such as be of the female persuasion, are simply something that has been sawed off on one by the will of God as so much clear evidence that those whom He loveth He chasteneth, and are to be regarded and dealt with accordingly, i. e., fed, clothed and walloped as occasion requires, and otherwise to be kept out from underfoot as far as possible. I hold this to be the view of common sense and reason, and there-

---

[68] The forcible ejection of Sewell Avery, Chairman of the Board of Montgomery Ward, from his office by members of the Army at the direction of President Roosevelt.

[69] See footnote 56.

fore your sentimental build-up of a parcel of naked young savages into a work of art strikes me as having a decided air of fictitiousness and unreality about it, eh, what? I don't take any stock in it coming from you, you see, because I've known you ever since the Mexican war as a sound, straight, experienced, hard-boiled gal with a big deckload of brains, and you can't make me believe you've suddenly gone squushy on the sacred joys of motherhood,—none whatever. Try that stuff on some one else; you can make a hit with it, all right, for you do it darned well, pretty as a picture; but me, I just larf hearty whenever I think of it.

In the matter of the refrigerator I have every sympathy with you. I tell you, the real trouble with gadgets is that they don't work. Lord, what a story I could tell about the infernal gadgetry on this place!—only nobody would believe it, because nobody in his right mind could imagine my putting up with it. The initial expense is nothing; it's the overhead that counts,—and does it count! If I had the money that has been fooled away on coaxing gadgets back into action since I have been here, you and I could treat ourselves to a three months spree at the Fritz-Carlton such as New York hasn't seen since the Gay Nineties. I get hot under the collar whenever I think of it,—but what good does that do? As Abe Potash would say, either you would be city folks or either you would be country folks, but you can't be both, —leastways, not in one house.

To Lincoln Colcord
NARRAGANSETT, September 1, [1944]

Congratulations on your summer. Ours has been a failure; vegetation burned to the roots in intolerable heat and drought. I am at Narragansett now where it has been even worse. I shall not stay; the region is overrun with naval officers, their wives and whelps, all uninteresting and the brats most objectionable. I shall go back to Canaan for a month and then strike out again, probably for Montpelier. With us there is no prospect of colour in the foliage this year,—all too long dry,—perhaps Vermont will show some.

Flaubert's correspondence, like most people's, is his best work. I doubt that any of it has been translated; at least I know of none. Mme Commanville brought out some volumes of his general correspondence, and other editors have taken a hand but the fool suppressions and expurgations which they indulge in are infernally irritating. Damn all these doting relatives and timid editors, why can't they keep their wretched meddling fingers off, and let a man's letters stand as written? I believe the letters to Mme Sand which you speak of come to us pretty much as is, and also the main body of literary criticism in his general correspondence, which makes it invaluable. To the common run of American readers, unfortunately, Flaubert means *Mme Bovary,* his poorest work, a fearfully laboured book, hard as nails, and repellent to a civilised mind. Getting through it was a great bore to me. Pater's view of it and Matthew Arnold's are quite correct, and we know well enough what Joubert and Scherer would have thought of it. When art becomes self-conscious it isn't art any longer, so if a writer sets out to construct a story in defense of some little private notion of literary art he cripples himself and his story never quite comes through. When Flaubert shook himself comparatively free and wrote *Salammbô,* for example, you had something by which it was really fair to judge his quality as a novelist. But better than all that, he was a capital critic of society as well as of literature, and I believe it is in this capacity that he will last longest; and hence it is his correspondence, which contains all his criticism, that stands the best chance of survival.

So you tell me the British H'embassy in Washington is perusing my *Memoirs.* I wish them joy of it. I am minded of the innkeeper at Chambéry whom Rabelais celebrates at the end of the Fourth Book. Look it up.

To George P. Bissell
NARRAGANSETT, September 2, [1944]

Thank you for the clippings. What a handsome record Franklin and his crew are leaving to revolt the historian!—a record of common liars and swindlers. We have had plenty of bad eggs in public office, but never anything like Franklin for brazen vulgarity in their misdoings, I am sure. When one remembers that he stands as a representative of our people one has a hard time keeping on the windward side of oneself. But there he is.

The shortening days depress me, as they always do. Like Goethe, my spirits are persistently low, and I am inert. The passage of the summer solstice sets one wondering whether one will live to see the turn of another winter solstice; not that in my case it matters much, for life does not owe me a red cent, but the thought crops up once in a while, and it is not animating. The reflection that one is doing something,—anything,—for the last time gives one an odd sensation. The other day, for instance, when I was looking over a lot of shirts it struck me that in all probability I shall never have to buy another shirt. There is a sense of emancipation about it which is pleasurable, especially with regard to places and persons, associations that have pretty well exhausted one's interest but that one keeps on with, more or less by the *vis inertiae*. Still, the thought is sobering, and a fit of low spirits keeps it to the front.

I have nothing amusing to tell you, except the inside story of the Dewey-Fish-Willkie incident. It illustrates the truth that almost any kind of professional can always wallop the starch out of the gifted amateur. It seems that the Republican regulars have been for some time trying to pry Hamilton Fish off his strangle-hold on his Congressional district, and thought that at last they had him beaten for the nomination. One day Ham dropped a casual word that he was sorry the Jews were so solid for Franklin; you remember his saying that. Well, Dewey, knowing that Ulster County is swarming with Jews, took the bait, hook, line and sinker,—darned if he didn't!—and solemnly read Ham out of the party on the "racial issue." Then Willkie instantly followed suit with his nickel's worth. What they either didn't know or didn't think of was that all Ham's Jews are summer people and don't vote! Even the boarding-house keepers are non-residents. So the consequence was that when the actual resident voters of Ulster County who hate the Jews like poison, got wind of what Dewey and Willkie were saying, they decided it was time for all good men to gang up regardless of party and vote for Ham; which they did, and Ham walked off with the nomination.

For some reason this tickled me immensely. I met Ham the other evening and rather like him, with somewhat the feeling I used to have towards Boies Penrose. Socially he is an amoosin cuss, like Artemus Ward's kangaroo. The very little I know about Dewey conduces to no respect for him. But his fate or Franklin's or any other job-seeker's counts for little in the face of the fact that the country's political destiny is in the hands of an ever-increasing inflow of humanity such as no other country wants and the devil wouldn't have.

To Elizabeth Lange

CANAAN, September 10, [1944]

I am just now home again after two weeks at Narragansett and a day or so in New York; so I shall cash your rain-check for you by way of a longer letter to read, if not a more interesting one. Nothing pleasant to report on my travels. Rhode Island is only a combination of an armed camp and a factory; New York is more than ever offensive at the end of a period of great heat. Filthy streets, filthy structures, filthy people; a lovely *ensemble,* stinking like thirty-seven regiments of devils! Spectacle and stench alike grow more nauseating with each day that passes, and isolation on this mountain-top grows steadily more pleasing.

My book-reviewing argues no interest but my liking to do it. I can say what I please, and it keeps me in practice at easy scribbling, with no sacrifice of time, labour or principle. I never thought of sending you my reviews, for they are not worth it. The books are amusing for their deadly seriousness and their complete futility, due to their writers' basic ignorance of what mankind actually is. But if ever you think you catch the scent of any highfalutin' social motive behind anything I do or say, you had better take another sniff and make sure it isn't something else. Maybe I have been too near a skunk, or maybe it is a reminiscence of some gal with whom I have been passing the time of day, but you can bet it isn't the rancid stench of the social consciousness. I have carried some pretty unsavoury fragrances in my time, but never smelt like Bro. Wallace or Harry Hopkins. By the way, speaking of smelly gals, why have they lately taken to dousing themselves with such fearful perfumery? Is it a symptom of war-fever, or what? I noticed it towards the end of the last war, quite as now, and I remember as a youngster in the time of the Spanish War the women went around stinking up the whole face of the earth with musk and patchouli. There would seem to be some connexion there, but I can't make it out.

Women are always complaining of men's disgusting habits, but I notice nothing ever induces them to give up their own; bathing in a tub, for instance, which is a filthy practice,—soaking in your own offscourings, then defiling your towel to get yourself dry, instead of coming out from a shower clean, like a decent Christian. Then in the matter of painting their lips red, most of the gals hereabouts are naturally a bit on the pale brown side, —drumhead complexion—and their faces simply won't stand the violent contrast. Then, too, they seem to think you never see the inside of their lips, as you are sometimes obliged to do momentarily, and the clash of the paint against the pale pink of the inner surfaces is a horrible sight. When you see it across the lunch-table, especially, it turns you from food. Twice lately I lost a good meal in that way; my appetite died in its tracks; and at that, the lady's face in its natural state would be quite easy to look at. Why don't you gals do some reforming on your own, by way of example? Why pick on us?

While away I read a couple of Somerset Maugham's novels with not much interest. They had no great action at their centre, and while he has skill enough, I think, to treat a great subject powerfully, (I am not sure that he has) I doubt he could also affect a reader delightfully, pleasurably; he certainly did neither in those two books which are all of him I ever read. So I hardly see wherein he is above the ordinary. The one modern writer who has made a really notable success of getting all the elements of permanence together in a story was Conrad, in *Typhoon*. The story centres on a great action which is never lost sight of; all the incidents are as strictly subordinated to it, and as skilfully, as in a tragedy of Sophocles. The treatment affects the reader powerfully and delightfully, and the more horrible the story becomes, the higher one's delight in it rises. So there you have all the requirements met in full and coördinated with superb skill. Conrad (as far as I have gone with him) never quite did this again, but to have done it once is enough to give him a place in literary history.

To J. Howard Rhoades

MONTPELIER, October 21, 1944

Your quartette started the season with a good programme, just about what I should expect. I wish I might have sat in on it. Some day you should let me hear what you can do with the Kaiserquartett. I know Schauffler well, a very amiable fellow with many pleasing enthusiasms and quite a number of sound ideas. I never read his *Musical Amateur;* perhaps I ought to look it up. My own experiences as an amateur would make something of a book, but somehow I feel no disposition to write one or indeed to write anything. Why try to share one's more intimate aesthetic or emotional experiences with other people? Let them enjoy their own in peace. If Stephen Foster, Nevin, Gershwin, fill their bill, why meddle with their taste? I see no reason. The most I ever did beyond mere occasional references was to write an essay for the *Atlantic* years ago On Hearing Good Music Done Badly, and that was harmless enough.

Twenty years ago I happened to be in Germany when for some reason there was a great general movement of resurrecting back-number second-string composers, people you hardly knew by name. It was a sort of revulsion, I suppose, from the craze for the fantastic in ultramodernity. It interested me to see what whaling big fellows some of those second-raters were, what a lot they did and how good it was, and how their only misfortune lay in their being overshadowed by their contemporary first-raters. A person who had the knowledge and the right feeling and could write well might make a stimulating and serviceable book on that subject. During that time in Germany I also noticed the singular attraction that Heine's drama, *William Ratcliff*, has for composers. Five that I know of,—and I never looked it up, so there may be more,—have built operas on it. I rather think that is a record, isn't it? I can't be sure, but as far as I know, it is.

The friend to whom I am most attached is thoroughly musical by heredity, taste and some cultivation, and he dislikes singing. So does Henry Mencken, who is even more proficient. They say singing offends them; much as I feel towards bagpipe-work, I suppose. I have wondered whether such people could become interested in the sheer physical phenomena of breath-control and tone-production like Gilibert's and Edmond Clément's; just as one is interested in the mechanics of prestidigitation or acrobatics which one might not otherwise care for. That in itself is an endless matter of wonder and delight to me; more so, I think, than any other element in vocal work, for I was never much moved by great voices, but by the quality of intelligence, taste and emotional power which the voice expresses. Where you have this coupled with a great voice you have a Battistini, a Selma Kurz; but at that, for me, the voice is the least of it.

I am up here for a little change from the bare countryside. I saw this small city for the first time last summer, and at once took a great shine to it. I shall stay until 1 November, and then dig in for the winter at Canaan.

P.S. I was interested in the historical side of the brochure on violin-collecting as "the aristocrat of hobbies." I can't get myself into the spirit of the hobby, for I never collected anything or accumulated anything that I could give away or otherwise get rid of. I seem to have been born with the belief that any kind of possessions are nothing but a headache, and I am thankful that I was; so I shall go out of life with very nearly as little as I brought into it.

To Bernard Iddings Bell

MONTPELIER, October 31, 1944

Have you ever begun a letter, then gone on maundering over wholly uninteresting matters without a word of what you intended first and foremost to write about? I did exactly that with the letter I sent you the other day. I rambled on about public affairs, for which neither of us cares a hoot in Tophet, when what I meant to do, first, was to lay you out for your remarks about Matthew Arnold. I'll bet you a new breviary against a cotton doughnut that you haven't read a line of Matthew since you left the seminary; and I'll double the bet that even then you never read anything but *Literature and Dogma*. I'm surprised at you you should talk that way, Mawruss. He left off writing poetry young: and I think his essay on Gray suggests a reason for it, and *a fortiori* for the fact which you quite properly observe, that the period is not marked,—and the present one still less, I may add, —by any superabundance of great poetry. But Matthew was the best of them, he and the unconscious Wordsworth; the conscious Wordsworth was terrible. Byron was a tremendous natural force in poetry, one of our greatest, perhaps our greatest, but always immature; Goethe's estimate of him is complete. Now for a preliminary penance, between now and Ash Wednesday, suppose you read Matthew's prefaces to his poems; his essays on Gray, Heine, Wordsworth, Shelley; and his essay on the function of criticism at the present time: and then recall what you wrote me and ponder your sins. I don't quite get what you mean by his inability to laugh at himself; his *Letters* show a light and flexible spirit, and surely *Friendship's Garland* shows a beautiful humour playing around qualities that are quite consciously his in common with his fellow-Britishers. No, me good feller, Matthew is not one to be disposed of in your cavalier fashion. I will go far enough to say that the thought of meeting or knowing him would not stir me; I shouldn't get on with him; but that means nothing, for I can't think of any British personage, male or female, ancient or modern, great or obscure, whom I would give two straws to know;—a matter of temperament predominantly French, I suppose. But you and I should be the last to disparage Matthew, for he was a sound prophet who always spoke out and always got it in the neck for so doing; e.g., read his Irish essays. How about it?

The other matter I meant to speak of, is the agnostic attitude towards *Father Malachy's Miracle;* thinking perhaps my observations might be of use to you in an illustrative way, as showing your nuns, etc., how well even an agnostic can accept the book and get satisfaction out of it. The agnostic rests on two principles; the first being that what we call a law of nature,—the laws of gravity, action and reaction, inertia, etc.,—is merely a registration of experience. He never loses sight of this. As far as he knows, for example, a body free to fall has always fallen down and not up; and this gives him a correspondingly strong expectation that free bodies will continue to do so. But he does not know of any *law* anywhere in the universe which compels them to do that, and he will not assume for a moment that there is one. This differentiates him from the type of scientific doctrinaire which makes that assumption. So when he is confronted by an unmistakeable break in the continuity of experience, like the prophet's floating axe-head or the flitting of a dance-hall, he has not the slightest *a priori* objection, is not in the least offended, and is perfectly willing to accept the fact.

His second principle is put in William of Ockham's formula that *Entia non sunt multiplicanda præter necessitatem*. The break in continuity certainly occurred, for there the dance-hall is, stuck on the Bass Rock; and the circumstances being what they were, the agnostic must regard the explanation offered as competent; and having no objection *a priori*, he is not offended; and there he stops. As for hypothetical inferences from the fact, he may or may not see something in them, according to the Irrefragible Doctor's "law of parsimony"; but his attitude towards the fact itself enables him to get thoroughly into the spirit of the story and gain a great deal of satisfaction and refreshment from it; as much, probably, as the most orthodox person, clerical or lay, will gain.

So when you are on the subject with your nuns and fellow-clericals, you might oncet in a while occasionally drop in a bean for the agnostic and tell them that he isn't such a bad fellow on the whole, when you get to know him. Aint it?

I hope to see you before too long.

P.S. You see how the above falls in with Aristotle's remark that fiction presents things as they might be and ought to be. The agnostic can't say but that the dance-hall might have flitted, and in the circumstances it should have done so. Hence his added satisfaction in finding that the story fills Aristotle's bill so nicely. Is all this too thin for you? I don't see why it should be.

To Lincoln Colcord

CANAAN, March 25, [1945]

So Bro. Vandenberg is going to see to it that the Polacks *get* their free democratic elections, is he? I'd be saying the same myself if I were in his place, for there are about 3½ million of Polish origin in the U.S.A., pretty well organised and full of beans about things in the old country. That means quite a little jag of votes. Bro. V. is from Michigan, and Detroit proper has one of the largest Polish colonies in America, while the population of Hamtramck, just outside, is 80% solid Polish, —a sort of industrial excrescence. If you ask me, I'd say Bro. Vandenberg is a vote-cadger of credit and renown, and is to be despised accordingly. He turned a flip-flop for the band-wagon at exactly the right moment, and is out for the nomination in 1948, or I miss my guess.

Did you notice the *Time's* report of the rural election over near Aachen? One of the fellows elected was a Nazi, or had been, and the word went out that he wouldn't suit the American occupation, so they held another election and dropped him. That was one of Winston's free democratic elections, only it just happened to be Franklin's, but it's all the same. It's the kind that Poland will get from Joe, if any, with love and kisses from Vandenberg.

If you want my opinion of Winston, Franklin, Vandenberg, *et hoc genus omne,* you might look up Kent's opinion of Oswald in *King Lear,* Act II, scene ii. It is a faint and far-off approximation to the content of my regard for these gentry, but I have found nothing in any literature that comes any closer.

To Bernard Iddings Bell

CANAAN, May 18, [1945]

All you need is the article in the eleventh edition of the *Britannica,* but be sure to get the eleventh, no other. The key to the position of Erasmus is that he was incapable of taking up with any but a sound cause, and in the contention of his time there was none such to take up with. He was like Falkland in the England of 1642, or like you and me in the dust-up between British and German imperialist interests. He could see that Luther's proposal to substitute the authority of a book for the authority of a pope was merely a proposal to change masters, and the practical outcome would be a Christendom of cantankerous sects and factions. Rome's cause was equally unsound, so there was no place for him in the fighting front of either army; no more than there is for you or me in the ranks of Fascism or Communism. "Scribes and Pharisees on the one side," as Chillingworth said of the Royalists and Roundheads, "publicans and sinners on the other." Or, as A. Ward put it to Lincoln, "Secesh in front of you and Abbolish at the back of you, each one of which is a little wuss than the other, if possible." Erasmus was for great reforms, fundamental reforms; and these were not to be had, no one could be interested in them, no effort after them could avail anything, they must be contentedly left to an indefinite future.

When one gets this view of Erasmus firmly established, everything in his career becomes easily understandable, straight-forward, luminous; and the *Britannica's* article is all one would want for the facts of his career. Perhaps, really, the less one reads *about* Erasmus, the better. Not long ago van Loon got out an issue of the *Praise of Folly*, with a very sympathetic Introduction, and he also made a great deal of Erasmus in *Van Loon's Lives*, which I like very much. The only academic work on Erasmus that I ever read was Emerton's, which I found most unrewarding. Erasmus is no game for professors or run-of-the-mill parsons, bishops and etcettery, *quia spiritualiter examinatur* as the blessed Apostle saith, and delicacy of insight seems rather a peculium of the scandalous and ungodly, for some reason, so maybe you had better take a look at van Loon.

I am just back last night from a week in New York, pretty well used up. What a place! What people! What a country!

To Bernard Iddings Bell

[RHODE ISLAND]
July 4, [1945]

MY DEAR LORD DUKE:

.   .   .   .   .   .

I am glad you found the right spot for a vacation. I came down here the other day pretty well shot up in one way and another, and I think with the change in

weather I am beginning to pull around. The season up
on the Mountain has been devilish. Tell Mrs. Bell I
don't believe Mexico has anything on us this year for
midges. I am covered with blains, scabs, scurfs, pock-
royals and pestiferous botches, and am 'arf out of my
mind with their ferocious burning and itching.[70] I rather
believe I shall stay here most of the summer, and seize
on a cool spell in August, if any, for a day or two in
New York.

To George P. Bissell

CANAAN, July 18, [1945]

Thank you for sending me the clipping. I know it
has not escaped you that our politicians and planners
are bearing down with all their weight on "full employment" after the war, instead of on production which
is the important thing. The answer is, of course, that
"full employment" is a first-rate vote-catcher, and if it
can be got only at the taxpayer's expense, no matter,
that's easy,—just appropriate $60 billion or so for under-
writing jobs, and the thing is in the bag. What un-
conscionable swine they are!

I believe I forgot to tell you that I was puzzled for
years by the reference to the "dead man's chest" in
Treasure Island. About a dozen years ago I learned from
Lord Frederic Hamilton that he too had been puzzled until he got the rights of it while he was cruising around
the West Indies. Somewhere among the Windward Islands there is a bare, flat, coffin-shaped rock with no
other land anywhere near it, and this is called the Dead
Man's Chest. I suppose it may have been used by pirates
for marooning objectionable characters; which probably
would account for the verse.

I too am by way of being marooned; heading for
Narragansett, where I shall be sequestered indefinitely.
I don't know what the trouble is, for I leave all that

---

[70] These were signs of his fatal illness, which he did not recognize. He ascribed them to insect bites. The terms used are from
Rabelais.

to the quacks, answering their questions and asking none. I always admired immensely Julius Caesar's great saying that life is not worth having at the expense of an ignoble solicitude about it. For some time, however, I have been really quite ill, feeble and worthless, and have now reached the point of letting the quacks roll up their sleeves and do their worst. One unpleasant aspect of the matter is that, like the knights of the Ringing Island, I am "bescabbed, bescurfed, all embroidered over the phiz with carbuncles, pushes and pock-royals," which make me indeed a loathsome object.

I'll keep you informed, or some one will, but I foresee I shall not be writing much at length. On his last day Lord Houghton said, "I am going to join the majority, and you know I always did prefer the minority." Witty fellow! I don't think much of the minority on the whole, but here and there there is one like yourself whom one wishes to stick by as long as one can.

To Bernard Iddings Bell

Sunday.
[July 22, 1945]

MY DEAR LORD:

Sorry, I can't do a thing. The quacks have got me down flat. They think it is some sort of systemic poisoning —they will know in ten days. All they are sure of is that it will be a long job in any case. Meanwhile I am incommunicado—can't read, write or talk—no energy for anything, so they keep me quiet, and I'm willing. Nasty business. I'll be anchored two months at least.

So forget all about me. I'll be with you in spirit, and will report progress now and then by postcard.

Ever of thee,
ALB. MAG.

To George P. Bissell

WAKEFIELD, R.I.
August 4, 1945

MY DEAR FRIEND,

The Supreme Court has handed down a final decision

that my trouble is the one called lymphatic leukemia—
any quack can tell you what that is, and when there
are no complications, which there aren't in my case, it
is not a killer right off the reel. It is simply devilish
to get on with.

It will be three months before I can pick up my correspondence. I am hived up in the doctor's clinic here,
and getting what I truly believe is the best attention
and medical care that I could find anywhere in these
days.

I am sorry you won't hear from me again for quite a
spell, but it does look that way.

Affectionately,

ALBERT JAY NOCK

per R.

To Lincoln Colcord

WAKEFIELD, R. I., August 4, 1945

I am sorry not to reply to your letter properly. It gave
me so much pleasure, but it will be at least a couple of
months before I can pick up my correspondence again.

I am down with lymphatic leukemia, which in my case
has no complications, and therefore is not too danger-
ous, but getting on with it is a very long and discouraging job.

My most affectionate greetings and every good wish.

MEMORIES OF ALBERT JAY NOCK
By
RUTH ROBINSON

MEMORIES OF
ALBERT JAY NOCK

THESE LETTERS, many of which were written to me, reflect the Albert Jay Nock I knew to a surprising degree. I do not suppose that I understood him completely, that I interpreted accurately those facets of his sparkling mind which gave light on many intellectual problems during the decades of our association, nor that the personality which warmed my life as only an intimate undemanding friendship can, was the only reflection of his temper. This cannot be a neat biographical sketch, complete with dates and circumstances of his whereabouts and concerns, full of anecdotes about his life with the great variety of persons who played important roles in his professional and personal development. I knew only a few of those people, I knew almost nothing of his projects unless they concerned me directly. As our relationship progressed from acquaintanceship to friendship, from occasional meetings to considerable periods in which we saw each other constantly, it was not accompanied by the usual coin of casual talk about family, other friends, other places, other ventures. We had been associated for some time, for instance, before I knew that Albert was married, that there were two sons of that marriage, that he had been—indeed still was, an Episcopal clergyman. He was ordained as a young man and served in several parishes before withdrawing from the ministry. Years later in April, 1924, he applied for renunciation of the ministry and the following October Bishop Herman Page of Michigan deposed him. Needless to say, Albert did not vouchsafe this information about his formal renunciation and it came to my knowledge very recently. His theological training added no mean measure to his intellectual stature. His knowledge of Hebrew, Greek, and Latin was a firm foundation for his superb English prose.

This reluctance to speak of his private affairs was not, I believe, due to secretiveness on Albert's part. I think that is borne out by the fact that one did not feel the curiosity about his personal affairs that often accompanies a growing friendship. As I have thought about him in the time that I have been preparing these recollections, it has seemed clear to me that the charm of his company lay in his absorbed concern with his companion of the moment. He had the rare quality of entrance into the immediate life and interests of his friends. There was no room for other people and other ways, they became extraneous and his concentrated attention on matters at hand precluded the idle prying question and the leading remark. If an acquaintance attempted to violate his sense of privacy, this is really saying his sense of propriety, he either responded with fantastic, confusing, soberly stated nonsense, or he answered so briefly and with such cold factuality that there were no more intrusive questions. He was not, in truth, concerned with the trivia of daily existence, with the small fact not applied to the greater truth, with the commonplaces of the usual. The gift of companionship is beyond value; we seldom find it, and it may be that its essence is the quality I am trying to describe in Albert.

His reserve as to his affairs was extended to his relationships with others. He was concerned with what a person was, what he thought, what he reacted to, what his abilities were, what he did with those abilities; that person's private life or private background did not interest him in the least. He was impatient with any attempt to provide him with the personal history of any one he was to meet for the first time. It is revealing that he admired Rimsky-Korsakov's autobiography; he said its excellence lay in the fact that the composer offered a profound analysis of his music and musical career and only said of himself that he was born and had a father and mother. Jefferson's restraint as to private matters certainly contributed to Albert's admiration for him and is reflected in his biography of Jefferson, which owes a good deal of its distinction to the fact that it is not written in the easy gossip-writer cum psychoanalyst approach of many biographers presently writing, but is a study of a great man's contribution to the many, rather than his private impact on a few associates.

It may be that Albert's indifference to the common exchange in human relationships is the reason his few excursions into fiction are not satisfying. The stories are not without emotional quality, but the protagonists are. He could create feelings, but he couldn't create characters. Once—that was when I first knew him— he told me he was planning to write a novel. As he talked about it, however, it became clear that not only would he not write it, but that he knew the novel was no medium for his ideas. He did once write a draft of a play with his associate on *The Freeman,* Francis Neilson. It was not without a mildly amusing quality, but after those who were given the manuscript to read responded with incredulity that they could have supposed it to be a play at all, no more was heard of it.

As I look back over the letters you have read, I am struck with the growth in assurance, in maturity in dealing with the world of affairs which he was just entering when I first knew him.

I met him by chance in the house of a friend.

One morning in the fall of 1909 an errand, what errand I no longer remember, took me to the apartment of Allen McCurdy, the minister of the Presbyterian church in Morningside Avenue. He was expecting guests, a man friend and a woman acquaintance, to join him for luncheon in an hour's time. The guests had not met before, he had clearly given some thought to his luncheon plans, and, unfortunately, his usually reliable housekeeper had failed him. Her daughter, very young and untrained and awkward, was in the kitchen. She might manage to prepare the food; she certainly could not serve it. That, I said, was no problem. I would play waitress.

The guests arrived, luncheon was started, and I, in the maid's apron and with what I felt was considerable professional style, handed around the food. As I offered the principal dish, the gentleman looked up and said, "Well, young lady, when you are through with whatever it is you are doing, why don't you come in and join us?" The host didn't look pleased at this turn of events, his carefully planned formal little party was taking on too slapdash an air, I suppose, and I retired in confusion to the kitchen. I firmly sent the girl in with the next course, but when the coffee was to be served she flatly refused to bring it in and I appeared once more with the tray. All pretense that I was the extra help had to be dropped, for I was drawn into the conversation. Explanations were made, Mr. Albert Jay Nock was introduced to me and I was presented to the lady who had been asked to meet him. Again I was asked to join the party, but I insisted I must leave, whereupon the guest of honor announced that he would escort me home. Perhaps he had not found the carefully selected luncheon partner sympathetic, or perhaps the little social occasion was too constrained. In any case, we left shortly. As we rode downtown he talked in his earnest manner about books. He recommended a book he was reading, and the following day left it for me at my family's apartment.

Albert was an immaculate person, even in those earliest days of our friendship when his clothes were likely to be worn to the point of actual shabbiness. I recall particularly a greenish threadbare raincoat which he kept until I protested one day that if he felt he could not afford to replace it with a respectable garment, no doubt a subscription could be raised among friends and colleagues for the purpose. He replied thoughtfully that his mother had made similar comments and perhaps he should discard the coat; it was not seen again, by me at an rate.

Nevertheless, he enjoyed dressing up on occasion, as if he were playing a part. He had an almost childish delight in a new garment, which often was obtained only after his friends complained about the one it replaced. Evening clothes were extremely becoming to him, as were the dark blue flannel suits he effected and the handsome corduroy lounging pajamas he wore about the house. For a period he had a pince-nez on a black ribbon and even, briefly, with great amusement sported a monocle he had acquired in England.

He was a finely constructed man, with small bones, hands, and feet. He was five feet ten inches tall, slight and quick in movement; he kept his excellent figure and carriage throughout his life. The salient expressions of his strong face were conveyed through his brilliant blue eyes, which could change instantly, be impenetrable, mischievous, or express great kindliness and sympathy. He had fair skin and high color and during all the years I knew him wore a mustache. His head was of distinguished proportions and, as he said himself, was "unusually high from the ears up." Long before his hair turned white, an iron-grey band at the edge of his brown hair was an outstanding characteristic of his appearance.

Such outdoor life as picnics, for example, meant only bugs and discomfort to Albert. Yet he loved long walks and he was a good tennis player when I first knew him, and he once told me he had been an enthusiastic and good baseball player in his youth. His other game was billiards, which he played a great deal at the Players Club in New York. He could amuse himself for hours at shuffleboard when on ship, but I don't think he knew anything of card games of any sort.

He was impatient with aimless social affairs and refused to be involved in any way in them; in the years after his distinguished position and editorial status were established he stoutly defended the seclusion and time necessary for serious writing. Yet he was no recluse and he had a wide range of acquaintances and friends in the great world of eminent writers, scholars, and statesmen. For example, one of his closest friends was Brand Whitlock, to whom he played the role of sympathetic mentor during Whitlock's distinguished career as a diplomat as well as earlier when Whitlock served in various political posts in his native state of Ohio, one such post being that of mayor of the city of Toledo.

Before the United States entered the first World War, Albert was commissioned by an American magazine to do a series of pieces on what was then the European War. He spent the major part of his time in England, Holland, and Belgium, and his observations fixed his opinions in regard to the inevitability of what was to come. He stopped off in Belgium to lend a hand to Whitlock, then United States ambassador to that country, and from Brussels he went on a mission into Germany on behalf of Edith Cavell, the English nurse who had been sentenced to death as a spy by the German authorities, to the shocked indignation of the world. Albert spent several hours with the German High Command, vainly trying to convince them of the sheer stupidity of executing Nurse Cavell. He never discussed the experience, nor would he talk of the tragic chaos the war had created in Belgium.

Undoubtedly his respect for German literature and art, and his comfortable ease in the German language, gave those years of war a peculiarly bitter flavor. He told me he was reared among Midwest German settlers and learned to speak German when he was a child. He never lost his facility in the language and he had frequently traveled in Germany. He felt a general sympathy with the German temperament and with the country, although there were distinctive German traits that he disliked.

Whether Albert acted in any official capacity in the Cavell matter, I do not know. He often had business in Washington at about that time. Whether this business had to do only with journalistic credentials connected with his trips to Europe, or he was given official or unofficial instructions for errands on behalf of Wilson's government he never said, just as he never made any comment about the reasons for the frequent Washington visits. His dim view of officialdom, which he expressed in anything but a dim manner, makes it hard to think of him in the role of an official person. He had friends who served the government in political jobs, certainly, but that never softened his attitude a whit. He said he had voted twice in his life, once at the insistence of a friend, and on that occasion he wrote in on the ballot the name of Cotton Mather who was, he thought, disagreeable enough to have been a bureaucrat. The other vote, he said, was for Wilson because he had promised to keep us out of war. How much of that was Albert's sardonic fun, it was not for me to say.

In the first year I knew Albert he spent the summer in Italy. He had said casually that he would write me from Rome, but there were no letters for some time. Presently, without explanation of the hiatus, letters began to arrive with frequency. I enquired the reason and he replied that he had been very ill. He said that he had had "Roman fever and the King and the powers that be put me under the King's physician. They did everything for me and I pulled through." He did add that he had been sent to Turin to recuperate and had become fond of that city, but that closed the subject and all further communications were about his travels and his enthusiasm over various regional opera companies and the Italian people.

When he returned he did vouchsafe that he had been decorated by the King; he had had "a rose pinned on him" as he expressed it, but he didn't think the title commendatore went well with the name Nock, so he decided to adopt the name Angelo di Angelis. He actually did carry the joke as far as to sign the name to three short stories he wrote at that period. Only one of these, by the way, was published. It is "The Puritan Heart" and it appeared in the *American Magazine.*

Except on his amusement at having been awarded an Italian decoration, he was so reticent as to the services that earned the honor that I have never known in what capacity the Italian government called upon him, although I am under the impression it was to enquire further into Albert's statements on the economic value of the single tax.

At some time, I think before World War I, Albert took a short trip to Russia—he said, just for fun. He wrote me from there, but unfortunately the letter is lost and I only remember that he went to a superb production of *Boris Godunov* and got some fine records.

Albert was no joiner in the interest of causes. He was, for instance, deeply interested in the economic ideas of Henry George and the single tax and spoke and wrote on the advantages of that system, but he was not a member of the group. "The only reform anyone is called upon to attempt, is the reform of one's self," he said. He believed an idea must remain free to change and develop.

The accounts of friendship cannot be cast up accurately as a column of figures, the stages of addition are not precise and one cannot recall how the sum of concern and sympathy and companionship was reached. I think the time when Albert and I became friends, not acquaintances, was during the following autumn after he returned from his stay in Italy. For some time I had found myself more and more discontented with the easy flow of my life. You must remember that those were the years which reflected the Tolstoyan influence; there was great fervor to save the world. I was deeply interested and wanted not only to work usefully, but to prove that I could earn my living, although it was not necessary to do so.

Albert was the first person I knew who understood why I felt as I did, and who could formulate my feelings for me, and find a place where I could be helpful. He introduced me to Fred Howe, Director of The People's Institute in New York, who engaged me to work on the Institute's programs. I worked for the Institute for several years, until the entrance of the United States into the first World War. My job, which was in connection with immigration, of course came to an end. I then spent much time here in the South County of Rhode Island until the war was over.

During those prewar years Albert held various editorial positions, contributory as well as administrative; when I first knew him he was an editor of the *American Magazine,* as were John Phillips, Lincoln Steffens, and Ida Tarbell. I remember his *American Magazine* colleagues called him "Nocko." I think it was at the Players Club that he was first called "A. Jay," the name by which he was to be affectionately known by most associates for the rest of his life. He contributed steadily to the *Atlantic Monthly,* edited by Ellery Sedgwick who,

Albert declared, was too fine an editor to reject his pieces, no matter how much personal suffering Sedgwick endured over publishing opinions so contrary to his own. When the *American Mercury* was founded Albert was invited to contribute. In the thirties his column, "State of the Union," appeared regularly for many years.

However, his work on *The Freeman* undoubtedly marked his editorial peak. Not only did he have a major voice in the continuing policy and contents of the magazine, but he was a founder, leaving the *Nation* when *The Freeman* was organized. Oswald Villard told me shortly before he died that he considered *The Freeman* the most distinguished periodical ever published in this country, excepting a single issue of a publication edited by his uncle, William Lloyd Garrison. A most generous tribute from a member of a family of editors and one who felt the loss to his own paper when Albert left the *Nation*. He went on to say ruefully that not only had Albert left him but that he had taken one of the brightest girls in the office with him, Suzanne LaFollette.

The Freeman was financed by Mrs. Francis Neilson whose husband was nominally the editor; Albert's stated role was that of coeditor. For the four years of the paper's existence, he tried to keep modestly in the background, and he insisted publicly and privately that it was Francis Neilson's publication. Neither the public nor his colleagues paid any attention to his denials. Albert Jay Nock was the editor of *The Freeman*, it reflected his editorial genius, and there was no use pretending it didn't. Although Albert said no more of the causes of *The Freeman's* demise than he did of his other concerns, he did tell me that he was exhausted by his administrative duties, a kind of work he found onerous, and that even if the paper had continued he would have withdrawn. Certainly there was an unhappy division of feeling among the staff and editors and Francis Neilson wrote an angry account of *The Freeman* in which he criticised Albert severely. I must admit that I did not read the Neilson pamphlet although it was widely discussed, and not to Albert's disadvantage. I had known Neilson as a charming, warmly sympathetic friend in earlier years, I knew Albert's invaluable contribution to one of the most distinguished journalistic ventures of this century. I did not want to read what I was assured was an ungrateful, false appraisal of that contribution by a former friend.

Albert once told me that during the years of the first World War he had turned to a rereading of Rabelais to escape the immediate realities of brutality and destruction. He said that this return to an earlier preoccupation had tided him over the war years and helped him to keep a balance of mind. He counted himself among the Pantagruelists from the time of his postgraduate work at Wesleyan University (Connecticut), when he and three cronies started their own little Rabelais Society. One of these students, Louis A. Parsons, known affectionately to the group as Zebe, became again, in Albert's later years, a frequent and cherished companion.

In 1922, when Albert delivered a series of lectures at a summer school Fred Howe established at Sconset, he met, as I did briefly, Catherine Wilson, an undergraduate at Vassar. She was a girl with remarkable intellectual liveliness and Albert discerned her great capacity for scholarly research. She subsequently continued her academic career at Oxford University, with her major interest centered on the fifteenth century. It was while she was still at Oxford that she began, at his request, the research which provided the scholarly basis for his writings on Rabelais. Their warm friendship and literary association continued for the rest of Albert's life and I think the value Albert placed on Miss Wilson's assistance is symbolized by the fact that he turned over to her all copyrights to the Rabelais material. Albert devoted about five years to his study of François Rabelais' life and work, with the constant assistance of Catherine Wilson. During that time he prepared a new edition of the Urquehart-LeMotteux translation of Rabelais. The introduction was published separately and in advance of the new edition, in which it was incorporated. At the time he was made a member of the Rabelais Society of Paris. After the years of hard work Albert announced that he was going to write an account of his many trips

through Rabelais' France, in lighter vein. I, too, shared
in the preparation of *Journey into Rabelais's France*. I
illustrated that book with a series of pen and ink draw-
ings; in this book three of us are represented. Yet I
did not meet Miss Wilson after the initial casual introduction at Nantucket, until after Albert's death. Here
again, you see, Albert's compartmentalizing of his life
and associations was in its usual rigid control. It has
been assumed, by the way, that the Letter to Cassandre
at the end of the *Journey* was addressed to me. It was
not. It is an expression of Albert's gratitude to Miss
Wilson for her devoted assistance.

I don't mean to infer that I knew none of Albert's other
friends and associates; many of them became valued
friends of mine, too. Hendrik Willem van Loon, Sir
Edgar and Lady Speyer, Suzanne LaFollette, Leonard
Bacon, William Briggs, A. E. Thomas, Walter Pritchard
Eaton, Amos Pinchot, Brand Whitlock, are names of
mutual friends that come readily to my mind, and there
were many others. Dr. Bernard Iddings Bell was another of Albert's most devoted friends whom I came
to know well and saw frequently. During the time that
Dr. Bell was warden of St. Stephen's College where
Albert received his B.A. Dr. Bell asked Albert to lecture there, which he did in 1930-31. Later, Dr. Bell became canon of the Episcopal cathedral in Providence and
he and Mrs. Bell came often to my house, especially when
Albert was staying here.

The number of letters and messages from Albert that
I mention may lead you to suppose that we were in un-
broken communication over the years of our long friendship. In one sense that is true, but only in the sense
I think that I was located in his mind, I was always
placed where I could be found. There were no extended
periods in which he did not write me from the country
he had gone to, or the city in which he found himself
in his excursions as a journalist. On the other hand,
I frequently had no notion where to address him, no
idea of the errand he was on, no knowledge of whether
he was traveling alone, with a party, or with a companion. At times there were reasons for communicating

with him, but it is a mark of his constant guarding of his independence that I had no idea how to reach him.

For that matter, I seldom knew where Albert lived. I wrote or telephoned him at the Players Club or the LaFayette. The LaFayette was an institution directed by Ramond Orteig in the great tradition of the coffee-houses of the eighteenth century. It was the constant resort of literary personages, theatrical figures, notables of the artistic world in general. The clientele was devoted and constant. Orteig served superb French food, there were accommodations to be had, for the LaFayette was nominally a hotel, and Albert often stayed there. But "The LaFayette" meant to its customers a superior restaurant which afforded a meeting place, a resting place, a place to receive mail and messages.

Albert had great distaste for any intrusion into his privacy, for explaining himself or his actions, or appearing to offer justification for any behavior that seemed reasonable to him. Whatever the reason was, I see in retrospect that the quality of the enigmatic in all his relationships, including those which endured decades of pressure and change and disappointment and success, was no small part of his fascination.

My first recollections of Albert are of a man of uncommon concern with the humanities. He was clearly the very antithesis of the commonplace in every expression, yet I remember feeling an uncertainty in his personality, almost a nervous hesitance in dealings with the world. His appearance was not unpleasing, but the handsome, distinguished figure he became in his later years was barely presaged; the commanding presence developed as his career developed. He was always disconcerted by any personal publicity, he was extremely modest about his literary achievements, and genuinely surprised when public honors came to him.

He was inclined to make light of most such honors. He once proposed quite seriously that the academic robes which were the symbols of various degrees awarded him should be cut up and put to other use; they were of such fine material, he thought it a pity to waste them. The two academic honors by which he set great store were the invitation to make the speech before the Rabelais Society at Johns Hopkins University marking the four-hundredth anniversary of Pantagruel, and the appointment to deliver the Page-Barbour Lectures at the University of Virginia. He properly regarded these as high honors, as well he might. He was indifferent for the most part to published criticism or praise of his books. The only resentments I ever heard him express were on occasions when he thought the reviewer was incompetent to deal with the subject matter. He was similarly irritated by the occasional person who seemed tiresomely empty and if he was cornered, he was capable of bating that person wickedly with the most outlandish statements and fables. After one such encounter, I said, "What do you do it for, to keep them from talking?" "Well," he said, "that is one way." Though he said that "men do about the best they can as a rule. It is mere delirium of egotism to expect more from them," he still found his hardest job in life was to suffer fools gladly.

Quite early in our friendship he visited me and my family in our house in South County from time to time, and as the years passed he became fond of this part of the country. The regional dishes, especially Rhode Island johnnycakes and brazilia, which is steamed salt cod served with boiled potatoes and much melted butter, pleased him very much. Albert liked simplicity in his daily life, but it was an aristocratic simplicity that suited him; plain but beautifully prepared food, informal households, but perfectly organized and quietly comfortable. He was irritated by flunkyism in those who served him and felt that his demands on personal service were only for things he could not do for himself. Nevertheless, he was impatient with domestic disorder and what he expected in his surroundings is harder to achieve than luxury, and that is unflagging physical comfort.

He was always on the defensive against having his time dissipated, however pleasurably, or his wits scattered. He composed in his mind. After intense mental concentration, sitting or lying perfectly still, he would often get up in his quick way and say, "Well, that baby's face is washed," or, "That's done, all but the writing." He wrote by hand with a fountain pen. His manuscripts rarely needed corrections or changes. His fine hand was considered difficult to read, but it was not, if you became accustomed to it. It had his characteristic orderliness, the orderliness of his mind, habits, person, all his belongings. He kept his possessions to a minimum, evaluating things by usefulness and quality. He had a great dislike of impedimenta, and he avoided cluttering thoughts as he did all other hindrances. When he came to the South County to write, I gave the word around that "the quarantine sign was out," so that he would not be disturbed and this led to his local reputation of unsociability. However, he was widely read in Rhode Island; *The Freeman* particularly had many faithful readers in the Providence area. He made many friends on the staff of the *Providence Journal* and frequently was invited to attend editorial policy meetings.

He was plagued with hay fever. He was in London when the allergy tests were first devised and he underwent a series of injections. Job was not more vocal than Albert over the results and he would never allow another allergy test. However, this trouble decreased as he grew older. He found the humidity of the American seaboard trying, but oddly enough the really fearful climate of Brussels never depressed him and he did some of his best writing there. He was fearful of minor ills and stoical in real suffering. At one time he was preoccupied with ill health and old age and his concern with these problems reached a climax in *Journal of These Days*. On one visit to South County he brought a copy of the newly published *Journal* and left it for a friend, Dr. Wilcox. The next morning the doctor telephoned and asked me to bring Albert to his office at twelve. Somewhat puzzled, we appeared.

"You know, Nock," the doctor said, "you had me reading all night to get to the end of your book. I was so afraid you would die before you finished that book of yours." No contemporary psychiatric tactic could have been more effective.

Brussels was his spiritual home. He often said he would

like to have lived in the France of the Second Empire and to have known Halevy, Offenbach, the Dumases, but the life of Paris in the years he lived in Europe did not attract him. Brussels was then a kind of clearing-house of European affairs; he was a member of the Cercle Gaulois, one of the great pleasures of his life, and there he met and talked with men of the greatest intellectual distinction and political wisdom. He knew the city intimately, from the Grand Place and its con-certs, tulip and bird markets, to the carnival grounds near the South Station. Many aspects of Belgian life pleased him, particularly the educated Belgian's high de-gree of culture and breadth of outlook.

Belgian standards of music in general, and opera in particular, were a joy to him. There are frequent ref-erences in these letters to concerts and operas he at-tended in many countries. He was a sensitive, perceptive listener. Long before it was usual to collect the records of great artists and compositions, Albert seldom returned from a journey to Europe without a few records of performers not yet known in this country; sometimes these records were of superlative performances of folk singers. I recall, too, that he had records of the singers of the Imperial Russian opera who did not appear out-side Russia.

He was delighted with the superb performances of Italian opera bouffe, the Mozart operas, and the gay French light operas, at La Monnaie in Brussels. Am-brosini, the director of La Monnaie for many years, pre-sented these works with an especial flair. Apart from their exquisite tunefulness, Albert enjoyed their reflec-tion of social life at its most brilliant period, their highly civilized art of treating grave matters lightly and light matters gravely.

In the last years of his life when Europe was inac-cessible, he spent much of his time on Canaan Moun-tain in Connecticut. There he lived in the seclusion neces-sary for sustained writing and there he wrote most of his *Memoirs of a Superfluous Man*. He was devoted to Vermont, too, and it was in Vermont that he began the *Memoirs*. William Briggs, the distinguished senior editor of Harper Brothers, persuaded him to write the *Memoirs*. He pressed Albert for some time before he agreed. Finally, one day Albert suggested that we drive over to spend the day with the Briggs family. When we returned Albert said dubiously, "Well, I guess just to stop Bill pestering me, I'll try what he says I can do."

Almost as soon as he began the book, he suffered what appeared to be a serious eye infection. Fortunately his eye doctor was spending the summer within easy distance, and on examination found that there was no more than a minor eye irritation which soon disappeared. Nevertheless, Albert went through a period of profound depression over the condition of his eyes because he was well into the first chapter of the *Memoirs* and had found that William Briggs' judgment was sound and that he was deeply interested in the project. From then on, he wrote most of his *Memoirs* in Canaan. The *Memoirs* occupied the greater part of two years. Albert stayed at Catherine Wilson's house for quite long periods during the writing of this book and again she was of great assistance to him, for she generously typed his manuscript for him. He always composed in longhand, and the typing of successive drafts was most important to him.

On August 26, 1943, he invited me to join him for luncheon in New York. He came in from Harper's with the first copy of *Memoirs of a Superfluous Man*. His heart had gone into this piece of writing as in nothing else he had ever written. As he handed me the book, he said, "I am very pleased and content, for I have said what I wanted to say." The outward control he was usually so successful in achieving under deep feeling is lastingly betrayed by the shaking of his hand that made what he wrote for me in this book almost illegible. The book had an excellent reception and happily he lived to realize its success.

He found Vermont an oasis in the summer months of the war years. "It seems farther away from what is going on, a place to wait," he said. He found those times uninteresting. "All human activities of any real character are subordinated to the dull and squalid busi-

ness of war." There was great talk of the Four Free-
doms and I recall his comment. "There is no such
thing, four or forty. Freedom has no plural. Freedom
either is, or isn't."

Late in June, 1945, Albert came to stay with me at
my home here in South County. He had been in Connecticut, up on the mountain at Canaan, but he had
been plagued by mosquitoes. He was, he said, badly
bitten and the bites were infected, and he could stand
no more; damp Rhode Island climate, or no, he would
come down to South County.

I was shocked by his appearance when I met him
at the train. The skin on his face and forearms was
covered with an angry rash, which he dismissed as being caused by "the darned little mouchettes." He was
pleased at being in South County again. All he needed,
he thought, was a salve from the local druggist to heal
the mosquito bites and a few days in the screened garden room of my house which he called "the cage" to
feel quite well again. I could not agree with such optim-
ism and after several days of prodding, he consented
to see a doctor.

He was always reluctant to consult medical men. Dr.
Wilcox, one of the few doctors in whom he had ever
placed reliance, had died. However, Dr. Malford Thewlis,
a nephew of Dr. Wilcox, was practicing in the vicinity
and he decided to see him. Certain findings in the examination encouraged Albert. His heart was sound, other
organs were healthy. But there was the question of the
blood count and that report must come from a labora-
tory elsewhere.

Albert decided to return to Canaan to get some of
his possessions. He had asked me if he might spend
the summer in my house and when I urged him to do
so, he said, "I must pack up some more things in Canaan
so that I can get back to work. I haven't had any energy
to work with." He returned after a few days, but not
to work, of course, for his physical condition deterio-
rated very rapidly.

Dr. Thewlis reported to me that Albert was suffering
from lymphatic leukemia and that he could not live more

than three months. What he originally told Albert, I do not know, but I remember that one day when I was starting out to do errands in the village, Albert asked me to have the doctor write the name of his disease down for him, and Dr. Thewlis reluctantly did so. However, Albert only commented that he had known a man who suffered from leukemia and that while it might be a nuisance, it was a disease of long duration.

During the weeks of his illness Albert had asked me not to notify his relatives or his friends, he didn't want anybody bothering him. As the lassitude that marks advanced leukemia increased, he was unable to answer the letters that came from friends, and I wrote notes for him at his dictation, but in no case did he confide his true condition. On the day the news of the end of the second World War came, I went to him and said, "I know it won't interest you much, but you might like to know the war is announced over." He said, "My dear, don't get your hopes up. If you live twenty years more, you'll be right on the verge of another war and may get in again, probably will. You aren't going to stop war until you change man."

Five days later, in the early morning of August 19, 1945, Albert died. He loved the South County and I think he was content to end his days here. I communicated with Canon Bernard Iddings Bell, and the Reverend Louis Parsons, both Episcopal clergymen and old friends. Canon Bell generously assumed the task of notifying the Nock family whom he knew. Albert had always said that he wanted to be buried wherever he died "without any fuss" and his sons agreed with me that his wishes should be obeyed. Canon Bell felt that there should be an Episcopal funeral service and he and Mr. Parsons came to South County at once.

The service for Albert was of the utmost simplicity. His body was placed in a plain coffin, which we covered with greens from the hills, and Dr. Bell read the service in the studio of my house. Albert is buried in the Riverside Cemetery, at Wakefield, Rhode Island. His grave is marked with a severely beautiful small stone of Vermont granite, which bears only his name and the dates of his birth and death. This stone was placed there by a group of friends with the permission of his sons.

The letters included here will, I think, make clear Albert's constant concern, not with the State of Man but the common estate of men and women. I have attempted no appraisal of his contribution to letters. I have not meant to write an introduction to a series of letters written long ago, but to introduce you to a man of exceptional discernment and intellectual force whose ideas have not lost their validity, nor their relevance.

RUTH ROBINSON

September 12, 1961
EDGEWOOD FARM
WAKEFIELD, R.I.